RETURN TO THE ISLANDS

ARTHUR GRIMBLE

RETURN TO
THE ISLANDS

LONDON
JOHN MURRAY
ALBEMARLE STREET, W.

First published 1957

Printed in Great Britain by
Wyman & Sons Ltd., London, Fakenham and Reading
and published by John Murray (Publishers) Ltd.

Even in a little thing
(*A leaf, a child's hand, a star's flicker*)
I shall find a song worth singing
If my eyes are wide, and sleep not.

Even in a laughable thing
(*Oh, hark! The children are laughing!*)
There is that which fills the heart to overflowing,
And makes dreams wistful.

Small is the life of a man
(*Not too sad, not too happy*):
I shall find my songs in a man's small life.
                    Behold them soaring!
Very low on earth are the frigate-birds hatched,
Yet they soar as high as the sun.

GILBERTESE SONG

TRANSLATED BY THE AUTHOR

CONTENTS

Contents

Illustrations and Sketch Map by Rosemary Grimble

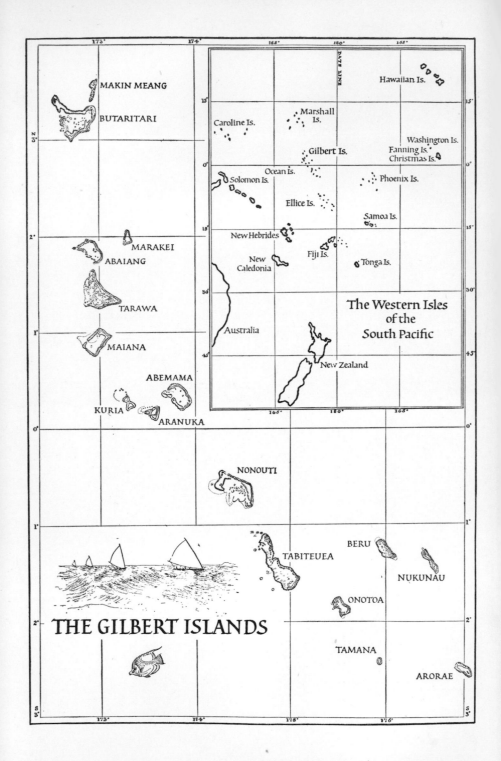

MAKIN MEANG

BUTARITARI

N 3°

Caroline Is.

Marshall Is.

Hawaiian Is.

DATE LINE

Washington Is.
Fanning Is.
Christmas Is.

Gilbert Is.

Ocean Is.

Solomon Is.

Phoenix Is.

Ellice Is.

Samoa Is.

New Hebrides

New Caledonia

Fiji Is.

Tonga Is.

The Western Isles
of the
South Pacific

Australia

New Zealand

2°

MARAKEI
ABAIANG

TARAWA

1°

MAIANA

ABEMAMA

KURIA
ARANUKA

0°

NONOUTI

1°

BERU

TABITEUEA

NUKUNAU

ONOTOA

2°

THE GILBERT ISLANDS

TAMANA

ARORAE

S 3°

In 1913, my main reason for wanting to join the Colonial
Administrative Service was that it would enable Olivia and me
to marry at once and set up house together in the remote, the
romantic Gilbert Islands. But in 1921, when our first long
leave in England was almost spent and we were up against my
return to duty, the relationship between our private life and
my service in strange lands did not look quite so happy. Our
four daughters had come into the picture by then, and the
climate of the Gilberts was cruel to growing children. If I
went back to my district out there, it was clear I must go alone
while Olivia stayed at home with the family.

The initial question was where 'at home' might best be.
We naturally thought first of where we were at the moment,
in a village of South Devon. But the Gilberts were anything
from nine to twelve weeks away from England in those days,
the variable factor being the time spent waiting for connections
in Sydney. So, if the family stayed on at Newton Ferrers, the
trip home to them for a three-months' stay, then back again to
my job, was going to need a grant of something like nine
months' leave of absence on full pay. The nice point about a
grant of that kind and length was that you took six years to
qualify for it.

Six years of separation seemed too much to pay for twelve

I

weeks of family reunion. We therefore turned to the alternative, a household exodus to Australia. With everyone in Sydney, less than two weeks away from Ocean Island, I could be sure of getting back to them on short leave for ten weeks at the end of every third year of service, and Olivia could visit me now and then for short spells, too. The only difficulty was that I would have to borrow about £800 to finance the move. Before plunging as deep as that on my pay of £600 a year I had to make sure of not being transferred out of the Pacific to a job on the other side of the world as soon as our migration was complete.

So I went up to the Colonial Office one day to collect that little assurance of stability we needed. Everything would have gone swimmingly, I'm sure, if my quiet and kindly opposite number, G. A. Jones, had been there as I expected. But he wasn't, and, as I had no appointment, it was in a way very courteous of whoever it was to see me at all. He was a smallish, sphinx-like person who sat very straight in his chair behind the enormous desk.

"Do you think I can count on being kept in the Gilbert Islands for three more years or, better still six," I asked him ingenuously, "if my service out there remains satisfactory?"

"*Remains* satisfactory?" he repeated with cutting emphasis. "*Remains* appears to stand for certain assumptions on your part. I wonder what they are?"

"Well," I faltered, "I thought my service . . . so far . . . I mean to say, I haven't earned any black marks so far, have I?"

"Haven't you?"

His question of course left me convinced on the spot that I had. My Resident Commissioner for six years, E. C. Eliot, had never been exactly reticent about my faults as an apprentice. I suddenly saw his confidential annual report (that sinister document never revealed in those days to the officer concerned) doing detailed justice to my every drivelling incompetence. But the shock of it made me argumentative. "If I've truly blotted my copybook," I urged, "why should I have been

2

appointed to act as resident commissioner for Mr. Eliot when he left for England?"

"I really can't say," he replied.

"But surely that was a mark of confidence," I insisted stupidly, "wasn't it?"

"Was it?"—his eyes were plainly gloating now, though his face was expressionless—"I couldn't possibly pretend to know."

I panicked on that line then and plunged panting back at the details of the family migration, the cost, the need of some kind of certainty, and so on. Looking back, I am horrified at the crudity of having tried to import personal emotions into Whitehall. But I still believed with all my heart in the idea of a paternally directed colonial service, and what I had to say meant so much to the family. The result was a babble of stumbling thoughts and stuttering words it still shames me to remember.

All that remained for him then was to finish me off neatly. "We know nothing officially of wives and families in the Colonial Office," he said. "We deal with officers in the field as officers, not husbands or fathers. And we never give guarantees not to move them from post to post, as and when we judge necessary."

The next day Olivia and I decided against the gamble of a migration. The question we had to answer then was: should I go back to the Pacific or resign and take a job in England? It was only up against this choice of ways that I learned for the first time how much our six years in the Gilbert Islands had put me in love, not with the people alone but, beyond them, with the colonial service as a way of life.

On the other hand, the way wasn't turning out very profitable for the family; also, there was a job waiting for Olivia and me in the West Country. A family friend, a director in a now famous hotel organization, was looking for couples like ourselves who might be put as learners in charge of small country inns and eventually promoted to bigger and better posts if they gave satisfaction.

3

We hadn't a doubt we could give satisfaction; it would be hard going at first, but soft compared with the life we had led in the Gilberts. Sitting on a green bank, high over the glimmering peace of the Yealm estuary, one evening of that divine summer of 1921, we said to each other, "Here's our way through. All of us together in England. Isn't it wonderful!"

Perhaps—who knows?—it would have remained wonderful for ever and a day if I had posted my letter of resignation that night. But I didn't. I found I couldn't write it just then, and when I sat down to it the next day, Olivia said she had been thinking. "You know," she said, "they would never have let you act as resident commissioner out there if there truly had been any secret marks against you. Why can't you forget that horrid little man in Downing Street?"

"Very good," I snapped, "I've forgotten him . . . so then?"

"Well . . . I've worried it out . . . you're the only old hand left in the Gilberts now, and there's a new resident commissioner coming along. Pretty rough on him if you don't go back."

"Why should I give a tinker's curse for him? We don't even know his name yet and we certainly owe him nothing."

"All right, all right," said Olivia, "but what about the Gilbertese? Not a soul but you left who knows a thing about them. You know what you're really thinking."

The letter wasn't written. Another went instead, asking for a second interview at the Colonial Office. The idea this time was to see if there was any chance of my being moved to a job nearer home after two or three more years of the Pacific. There must be someone there—some great and gentle power at the top—we felt sure, who could see that we were helped at least to that extent. By heaven! I said to Olivia, I'd resign on the spot, I would, if I couldn't get through to whoever it was. I kept on repeating it to myself all the way up to London.

But it was J. F. N. Green, tall, silver-haired and gently courteous who received me this time. Young men of my generation didn't easily explode into resignations with seniors

4

of his calibre. I think he must have heard of my massacre by the other man, for he opened with masterly kindness, "I've been wanting to meet you, Grimble. We have it on record that you performed with credit as acting resident commissioner out there of late, and it looks as if we shall be asking you to hold the fort for us again, until Eliot's successor arrives. Now . . . tell me your troubles."

Gracious, sagacious, Mr. Green! That single pair of words, 'with credit,' was instant balm upon my mutilated vanity. I said my piece then without too many stumbles. He listened with care, helping me often. He minced no facts, though, in his answer.

Outside the 'closed' services of Malaya, Ceylon and Hong Kong, which were entered through the doorway of competitive examinations—he told me—promotions and transfers in the colonial field were largely a matter of chance. "They are being wretchedly mishandled here in London, there's the truth of it," he admitted. "They always have been. We of the geographical departments can't honestly guarantee anything to anyone. We try to look after our own men; I will see that your name goes forward; but—I'm sorry—I don't know when you can hope for a move, if ever, or where to."

As for wives and families, he went on, something was now being done to recognize their official existence in Africa. But the African colonies had the money; we in the Pacific were too poor to pay for improvements; we were the backwater territories—the Cinderellas of the Empire, as he put it.

"Then perhaps it would be best, after all, to borrow £800 and take the family to Sydney, sir," I said forlornly, when he had done.

He thought a long while before he answered. "No. I wouldn't say that. The whole thing's a lottery . . . but you may be one of the lucky ones. Don't in any case load yourself with a big debt at this stage of your career, my boy."

I wish I could think that, even without that final, fatherly 'my boy,' his word of praise and crystal clear candour—too

5

kind to deceive me with any false hope—would have sufficed to hold me to my job. After all, it wasn't my service that had failed me, only my master, and the blame for whatever disappointment I felt on that score lay mostly at the door of my own romanticism. It simply wasn't possible for any official automaton like the Colonial Office to have the kind of collective heart I had expected of it. I did see that at last. But I had a doleful vision while he was laying such heavy emphasis on internal mismanagement.

I seemed to see, down the vista of the years ahead, an endless procession of forgotten servants trooping in to Downing Street from earth's far corners to ask, as I myself had asked that day, "What about me?" only to be answered with the courteous vagueness of kind men endlessly impotent: "Sorry ... we know the fault's at this end ... we do feel for you ... but there it is ... we can't do a thing about it."

The thought goaded me within an ace of leaping to my feet and throwing in the sponge before he had finished speaking. It was, in very truth, only that final 'my boy' of his, as friendly as a candle in a haunted room, that held me to my service.

Olivia and I decided to drop the idea of inn-keeping. The only money I borrowed was £150 to keep the family in funds until I got back to my post. I sailed for the Pacific, via Australia, alone in an emigrant ship, towards the end of September, 1921. It was to be seven years, not six, before I saw the children again but half-way through that time Olivia inherited a small legacy and splashed it on a fifteen-months' visit to me out there.

On the way out an A-deck passenger, a widowed lady who owned a public house in a Melbourne suburb, offered me a job as barman's assistant there. She said she had been keeping an eye and an ear on us emigrants below decks and fancied she could make something of me if only I could get rid of my lahdidah Pommy accent. I was ready to discuss practically any possibility by that time, but when I began bargaining for better pay and perks than she had mentioned, she peremptorily withdrew her invitation, and a fellow-emigrant in No. 2 Hatch eventually got the job. From that time on to the end of my official career not a soul in the world of big business ever again showed the slightest inclination to tempt me with offers of employment away from the colonial service.

I

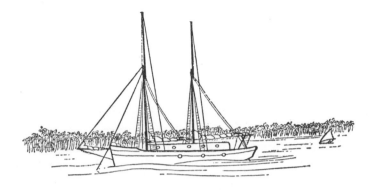

Friends in Exile

After only a fortnight's wait for a ship in Australia, twelve days
at sea from Sydney to the equator saw me back at Ocean
Island, the capital of the Gilbert and Ellice Islands Colony,
in the almost record time of nine weeks and five days out of
England. They told me when I arrived that Herbert Reginald
McClure, a senior district commissioner from Kenya, was
going to be our new chief. As he and his wife were due to
appear about three months from then, we had to get busy at
once putting the residency into shape for their coming.

The residency was wonderfully sited next to our cricket
field, on the edge of the island's high plateau, three hundred
feet above the burnished immensity of the sea. Perhaps partly
for that reason our late chief, E. C. Eliot, had borne patiently
enough with its leaking iron roof and sagging floors. But,
beyond this, his previous service in the grim political school
of the West Indies had taught him to have modest notions
about the housing of public servants. We doubted if the
McClures could possibly have acquired such enlightenment
as his in darkest Africa. So we decided that the repairs must

be radical; and this meant, for one thing, that I couldn't occupy the house myself while acting as resident commissioner. But I felt no hardship in forgoing that little bit of grandeur, because the Methvens asked me to stay with them instead.

Six-foot-four Stuartson Collard Methven was officer in charge of police and prisons, Ocean Island. He functioned in addition as superintendent of public works and public prosecutor in the weekly magistrate's court. We took it for granted that he would also operate, whenever the need arose, as foreman of works and sanitary engineer, immigration officer and customs boarding officer, chief landing waiter, chief store-keeper, and principal plumber, government station. We just didn't count the hundred other odd jobs, unsavoury chores, emergency duties and impossible tasks that his kindness undertook as a matter of course for the daily comfort of the seven households that made up our small official settlement on top of the island.

Stuartson and Ruby Methven had been close friends of Olivia's and mine ever since the day of tremendous surf in May, 1914, when, as new arrivals from England, we had been snatched from our plunging ship by Stuartson with his perfect boat's crew of Ellice Island policemen and brought gasping to shore through the charging combers of Ocean Island's boat passage. It was heartening to look forward to a few months of their companionship before going back alone to tackle life on some out-station of the Gilbert or Ellice Group.

There was Ocean Island's wonderful mail service, too, for comfort. The big local mining concern known as the B.P.C. —otherwise the British Phosphate Commissioners—was at that time exporting over 300,000 tons annually of the island's fabulous phosphate of lime deposits to Australia or New Zealand. The forty or more ships a year that this brought to us from Sydney, Melbourne and Auckland meant letters from home at least twice and often three times a month.

By contrast, three mails a year was the average expectation

in any of the other twenty-four Gilbert and Ellice Islands. That seven-hundred-mile chain of dreaming atolls to east and south of Ocean Island, strung so remote across the equator through the deep heart of the Pacific, had little in it to attract freight-hungry shipping from the outside world. After feeding its own lagoonside populations of thirty-odd thousand souls, it could put up no more copra for export than a single medium-sized tramp a year could carry away. The only other ships that paid regular annual visits were the s.s. *John Williams II*, doing her twelve-monthly tour of the groups for the London Missionary Society, and a recruiting vessel sent round by the B.P.C. to collect Gilbertese workers for Ocean Island. Under those conditions, your mail, when it did arrive, was certainly a big one. You could squeeze some extra fun out of it, too, after swallowing the lot at a single delirious first session, by putting all the letters you wanted to see again back through the local post, so that they reached you at breakfast, one every morning, for several weeks on end. But three, or four, or possibly even six months at a stretch is a long while to wait for home news, and I needed the preliminary breather fate had given me with the Methvens before going out alone to face it.

What I did miss at first on Baanaba (that was the Ocean Islanders' own name for their lovely little home) was the gay and spontaneous mass-friendliness I had learned to expect from villagers over in the lagoon islands. The eleven hundred Baanabans were a good deal shyer by nature than the other, bigger Gilbertese populations. Also, the growth of the phosphate mining industry, with its self-contained European settlement of fifty or so engineers, clerical workers and artisans—half of them married men with families—did establish conditions in which the white man and the brown, each contentedly absorbed in the fullness of his own domestic ways, tended to meet each other seldom except in the relationship of employer and employed.

11

Nevertheless, if you took the trouble to go calling in any of the four exquisite Baanaban villages—Tabiang, Uma and Tabwewa by the sea, or Buakonikai (meaning 'Place Among Trees') on the island's crest—you could always count on having a cluster of friends around you within a very few minutes of your arrival. Your best time for a visit was about five in the evening. All the world was at home then, the men just back from fishing, stretched at ease within the open-sided houses: the women outside, under the high-arching coconut palms, getting their earth-ovens ready to cook the day's catch; the golden-bodied children at play where hibiscus and poinciana burned between the grey-brown thatches. In that tender hour before sunset everyone's tongue was loosened, whether for serious discourse or joyful gossip, as at no other time of the day. I learned to depend much for inward peace upon the evening calls I paid in the villages. And then there were the visits with which 'Movement of Clouds' of her goodness honoured me.

Movement of Clouds (Tebutinnang in Gilbertese) was the only granddaughter of the headman of Tabiang village. She and her grandmother Tearia had been particular friends of mine ever since my greenest cadet days on Baanaba. It was old Tearia who, back in 1915, had taught me—while her great mane of silver hair was being brushed by the little girl—my first steps in Gilbertese myth and legend. But even earlier than that, Movement of Clouds, a naked elf of only seven at the time, had shown me how to belch with decorum, as every good guest should do, in thanks for hospitality received.[1]

Though I had spent most of the six years that followed away from Baanaba in the lagoon islands, she had been at pains, whenever I had reappeared at headquarters, to re-entrench her position as my accepted authority upon how true Gilbertese ladies and gentlemen did—and I myself always should—behave while visiting or receiving island friends. I had dubbed her for

[1] *A Pattern of Islands*

this purpose *Nei Kaeti-kawai*—meaning Female Straighten-ways or, broadly, Girl Guide—and she was delighted with the title.

Her approach to the business of keeping my manners up to the mark had never varied through the years. Wherever I happened to be staying, she would call on me (dressed, alas, in her most heavily flounced Mother Hubbard) within an hour of my arrival and wait in the back premises, often for as long as three or four hours, until I was ready to receive her. Sitting then on the mat by my easy chair, she would solicit my favour-able notice of the wreath of white flowers she had plaited and was wearing in my honour. It was up to me to exclaim in response that it looked on her small dark head as lovely as an aureole about the brows of Nei Tengaina, virgin spirit of the dawn—which I honestly felt it did. Having considered which with grave pleasure, she would plunge into a masterly résumé of the points of etiquette she had collected for me since our last meeting. When that was done, she would accept with courteous grace a bowl of brown sugar and water from my hands, drink it off, return the vessel to me while eructating with exquisite punctilio for grace after meat, receive my thanks for her help, and go her way fulfilled.

One of my earliest calls after arriving back from England was on Movement of Clouds' grandfather. It was not a social call: I had some official business—I forget what—to discuss with the old man as headman of Tabiang village. So I planned to be there soon after 3 p.m. At that hour, I guessed, his wife and granddaughter would probably be busy shopping (or even busier gossiping with shoppers) at the B.P.C.'s big trade store down at Uma, and he sitting peacefully alone in his brown lodge, just emerged from a refreshing afternoon nap.

But my calculations turned out wrong. Tearia and Move-ment of Clouds were both at home with him and all three were heavily engaged with another caller. This last was a large brown mission teacher dressed in the trailing white waistcloth

14

and starched drill jacket of his calling. He sat crosslegged on a
guest mat in the middle of the floor, surrounded by the other
three, who listened, dumbly sweating in the languid afternoon
heat, while he stated the official reason for his call.

They were all so absorbed in his business that nobody
noticed me picking my way down the hillside through the
palm stems. Rather than interrupt their session, I joined an interested little audience gathered in the shade of a mighty bread-
fruit tree near by, and listened in.

It appeared that two village policemen had started the

trouble. Those interfering fellows, the teacher said, had come snooping round his back premises last night, looking everywhere for a certain pig of his. Having failed to find which, in its pen or anywhere else, they had asked him what about it. And when he had replied *Kai ngkam!* meaning he neither knew nor cared, they had said what a pity, had written his name in a book, and told him he must appear before the Native Court next week on a charge of neglectfully permitting his pig to wander, for which crime the prescribed fine was sixpence, or, at the option of the convicted party, twenty arm-spans of coconut fibre string. And when he had said how could they accuse him like that of a wandering pig when they had seen absolutely no pig of his wandering anywhere, they hadn't had a word to say in reply. And the whole set-up was a shame that stank to Heaven, anyway, because it was clear to every Christian that missionaries, together with all the village teachers, pastors and deacons who assisted them, being representatives of the Almighty here below, should by rights be treated as immune from the action of the silly, treacherous, oppressive and altogether ungodly man-made laws for which the headman and his police minions stood.

Never had prelate of old, I felt sure, claimed benefit of clergy with arrogance more self-assured than this simple brown lay teacher's. But never, on the other hand, have I heard officialdom's majority views about itself more confidently stated than in the old headman's immediate reply.

"Stuff and nonsense!" he bawled, leaping to his feet and pointing at his visitor: "Stuff and nonsense, calamitous gaby! It isn't you missionaries who are above the law . . . it's we of the government . . . we, the lawgivers!" Not even a Treasury spokesman in Whitehall could have bettered the insolence of it.

Yet even in that moment of superb affirmation, the cagey personal modesty of the trained official overtook him. In saying 'we,' he hadn't meant to claim that he himself made any laws, he paused to explain laboriously, sitting down again;

only, being a village headman made him a colleague of the shining company who did so—the resident commissioner and his galaxy of district officers. Now there, if the teacher was looking for heavenborn masters, was a gang worth serving. Why, they walked practically arm in arm with the Almighty the whole day long!

And then his burning *esprit de corps* ran away with his tongue again. If only the teacher could see us at work, he said, . . . the divine play we made juggling with our own laws . . . the way we would be honouring them one day, ignoring them the next . . . the way we would be adding, revoking, twisting this way or that, with never a by-your-leave to missionaries, or native governments, or anyone else in earth or heaven, or even to the spirits of the underworld—well, if only the teacher could watch us at all those activities, he said, he would realize what truly heavenborn creatures we were . . .

He had clearly reached the top of his form at that point; anything more would have made anticlimax. I hurried down the slope to stand under the eaves of his house, a hand laid on the edge of its raised floor, begging admission. He simply had to stop then and welcome me: "You shall be blest, Kurimbo [Grimble]. Enter . . . enter."

All were silent as Movement of Clouds, on hands and knees, dragged a guest mat across to where I could sit on it propped against a corner post. She sat beside me crosslegged, holding my hand while I pronounced the ancient formula of courtesy she herself had taught me, "Blest be this house and everyone within." It was plain from the way her enormous eyes shone up at me that she was prouder than ever to have the privilege of being the instructress and friend of a creature so celestial. And alas, I said nothing to disabuse her innocence.

A little breeze was born like a cool thought in the heart of the forest. I remember still how soft, as we settled down to gossip, the sound of the surf a hundred feet below came filtering up to us through the rustle of the palms. There was no more striving between Church and State in the wistful calm that fell upon us then. As far as I know, the case of the wandering pig was never brought to judgment.

But I was puzzled about Movement of Clouds when I got home. Though her welcome that day had seemed to mean she still valued our friendship, she had not once come to see me since my return from England. So, when three days had passed since my visit and yet she had not appeared, I wrote begging her to pity me and call. At nearly fourteen she had already had six years' schooling with the Sacred Heart Mission at Tabwewa and was well able to reply in her own language.

Her neatly written letter arrived two mornings later, I have it still. I have altered nothing in translating it except for here and there putting in a comma of my own:

> Kurimbo, my loved uncle,
> You shall be blest.
> Be thanked for your letter, Kurimbo. My heart was glad to receive it but heavy also because of many things.
> See here, Kurimbo, I am a grown woman now. I became ready for marriage many moons ago when you were in Engiran [England].
> And now my grandfather is considering a husband for me to marry when I am fifteen years old, and you are not really my uncle, and I can never be much alone with you again.
> But I have a thought which is perhaps lucky, perhaps not. I will be with you at five o'clock this evening and disclose it.
> We shall meet, Kurimbo. You shall be blest. Remember me with love.
> Me, your unhappy Straighten-ways.

I waited for her on the broad front verandah of the Methvens' house near the police barracks. She arrived on the tick of five as delicately garlanded and goffered as ever. She did not

ask me to admire her beautiful white wreath of *uri* blossoms
as she settled herself on the guest mat; but she did greet me
with a wan smile, and when I volunteered the time-worn compliment about the Dawn Virgin's aureole she laughed: "How
sad my heart, Kurimbo, if you had forgotten to say that
today!" And then, all at once, the melancholy fell off her like
a shed cloak and she was a child again.

It was only after ten minutes of the old kind of gossip mixed
with talk of my four daughters, whom we always called her
little sisters, that she came to the 'thought' she had mentioned
in her letter.

"You remember the words of my grandfather?" she suddenly asked me: "When he spoke of the games you and your
Old Man can play with the law? When he said you can make
it and undo it, just as the fancy takes you, up here on the top of
Baanaba?"

"Yes ... but look here ... " I began anxiously.

Her eagerness swept me aside. "What a wonderful power
is that!" she went on, her eyes lifted to mine. My heart rose
up in pride as my ears listened; and then she whispered to
me, "Now that Kurimbo himself is our Old Man for a time,
who is there to prevent him?"

"Prevent him ... I mean me?" I repeated blankly. "Why
... whatever from?"

"From changing the law, Kurimbo," she said, with a kind
smile for my obtuseness.

"In Heaven's name, what law?"

"The law of marriage."

"But why should I want to go changing the law of marriage
all of a sudden?"

"For love of me," she answered simply. "Please, Kurimbo
... this husband they are going to tie me to is a nice boy ... I
like him ... but I don't want to be engaged to anyone yet. I
want to come and go without care. Can't you make a new
law about it for my sake?"

"You mean a law something like this, I suppose," I said

with laboured irony: "'Everyone in the world is forbidden to get engaged, or try to get engaged, to the girl child Tebutinnang, otherwise known as Kaeti-kawai, until she says she is willing to be tied; and anybody who breaks this law will be put in prison for six months.' Would that suit you?"

She glowed with pleasure. "That would indeed do nicely," she replied with a quick, excited laugh, "except that I don't think anyone ought to be put in prison for just trying."

My momentary irritation faded. Pity and shame overwhelmed me. I confessed with hanging head then that the Old Man and district officers like me were nothing like the all-powerful lawmakers her grandfather had pictured us.

In earlier times, it was true, things had been different, but nobody nowadays could interfere with the Gilbertese marriage laws as she expected me to do. It wouldn't be right . . . and so forth . . .

The happiness was drained from her face as I stumbled on. I cursed my thoughtlessness as her hurt gaze clung to mine. No more than a little word from me after her grandfather's big talk in the village would have sufficed to spare her this piteous disenchantment. "I am sorry . . . sorry . . ." I mumbled and waited, clay-footed idol I had proved, for her reproaches.

But she said not a word, only looked at me in silence while her slow tears gathered. I miserably watched them well up, fat and shining, one by one, roll down her cheeks, meet at her quivering chin, and tumble thence in sorrowful rain upon her lap.

Nevertheless, though my vanity had let her down so badly, the thought did break in on me soon that all was as yet far from lost.

"Cheer up, Straighten-ways," I recovered voice enough to say. "It's true I'm not a god, alas! It's true I can't be your real uncle. But what about you? Have you thought what you and I can do about it?"

Still she said no word. But the tears ceased to flow, and a small hope dawned in her eyes, as she waited for more.

"Five years ago, at Tarawa, a little girl of Betio village took the name of my eldest daughter, Joan; and Joan she has been ever since. So what relation is she of mine, would you say?"

She wiped her wet cheeks and blew her nose with sudden gusto on the handkerchief I tossed to her: "That girl is your daughter's name-sister, Kurimbo."

"And what duties does she owe me?"

"She owes you all duties that a daughter owes you, until she dies."

"But suppose she gets betrothed to some nice young man. Can custom not prevent her then from coming to see me?"

She drew herself across the floor to where my right foot rested, and laid her hand upon my brown brogue: "No, Kurimbo, not even then."

"Very well. Do you remember my second daughter's name, or have you forgotten it?"

"It is Roti-mé-ré," she murmured, arranging and re-arranging my shoelace with gentle fingers: "A beautiful name . . . none in the world more beautiful."

"Good. Nobody has taken it yet. Would you like it for yourself?"

She bent her head so low, I could hardly catch her whisper: "I would it were mine, Kurimbo." Then she picked up my shoe, complete with foot inside, hugged it to herself and laid her cheek upon the toecap.

It would have been a pretty gesture had things rested there—which is to say, had my foot remained at the approximate level of her chest as she sat upon the floor. In that position, my leg stuck forward at a reasonably dignified angle from the chair I sat in, and I could undoubtedly have regained eventual control of it without great loss of face if Ruby Methven had not chosen that particular moment to arrive home from a visit to friends.

The polite child sprang to her feet as soon as she saw Ruby and this again, *per se*, was a graceful act. But, for some reason I could never divine, she forgot to give me back my foot as

21

she sprang. The result was that Ruby's first view of me was flung back in my chair with one leg wildly cocked up against my little friend's bosom.

"What . . . playing at circuses?" was all she said as she passed us, to disappear upstairs, which struck me as very unsatisfactory. But when her idiot laughter came ringing from above Straighten-ways dropped my foot with a crash and followed suit; so I suppose I was wrong to remain annoyed.

Two weeks later, there was a big ritual in Tabiang village, to turn the name Tebutinnang into Rosemary. There simply had to be a ritual, her grandfather said. You can't be too careful with a new name. A name's a thing—a substance: evil spirits love to burrow into it, as termites into wood; and once they're in, it's done for. Your only salvation then is to throw it away quickly, quickly, before they have eaten the heart out of it. If you don't, you will wake up one night to feel your own heart too being gnawed away to nothing. But you're safe enough from horrors like that if your grandfather knows how to put a name on you properly.

The first step in the ritual is to make a safe enclosure to protect the new name and its prospective owner from the very outset. So there in Tabiang on the chosen day—at the sun's high noon, his supplest hour for magic—Tebutinnang's kinsfolk were gathered around her. They sat shoulder to shoulder in a closed circle, mother's people on the south side, father's on the north, facing in towards the little girl at their centre, while father's father walked round inside the ring dropping whispered words of power like a kind of elastic web-fence between them. Thus reinforced, the human rampart would stay impenetrable to any kind of earth spirit, no matter how the children wriggled out of line or the adults twisted in in their seats thereafter.

It only remained then to provide against the spirits of sea, sky and underworld. The sign of a magic solar cross, stepped out within the circle, easily did that. Intoning his powerful spell as he went, the old man strode first from north to south and back again, himself the sun in its yearly course from solstice to solstice; then from east to west and back again, the sun this time in his daily rising and setting. And behold! (as he said to me afterwards) a roof of safety and a floor of protection for the sanctuary were complete.

I felt bound to tell him that the one magic formula he had used throughout, though very beautiful, seemed to me almost too simple to achieve the results he claimed for it—

> Off with you, spirits of fear, spirits of death!
> Give way to the sun and the moon,
> For this is a sanctuary,
> This is a place made safe.
> Blessings and peace upon us,
> Blessings and peace.

"Yes," agreed the old man, "it is only a little thing. But we put our whole trust in it and also in the power of the sun and moon to protect us: so it works for us according to our heart's desire." Which seemed to me quite good sense in a pagan and a bureaucrat.

So there, her sanctuary perfected, sat the grave little girl within it, her new name alive in her heart. Alive but hidden; for, even in that safe place, it would be unlucky to speak it aloud before the old one had been properly discarded.

The throwing-away ritual started as soon as we began to tuck into the feast. The feast was, in fact, an integral part of it. As the women brought round portions from the stockpile collected within our circle, grandfather came prancing in their train to snatch titbits from our very mouths and, amid hoots of laughter, fling them to the spirits outside. The dull, ordinary dishes like bully beef or sweet potatoes didn't attract him. He went for the real treats, such as fish heads in molasses and sardines mashed with strawberry jam. North, east, south west he hopped and pounced in turn, scattering those delicious fragments until the grass outside was filthy with them; and, as he scattered, he bawled:

"Here, you spirits of earth!
Here, you spirits of heaven!
Here, you spirits of ocean and the underworld!
Here is your food, the name,
Even the name Tebutinnang—o—o!
Is it tasty, ke-e-e? Stay outside and eat it.
Stay outside for we are throwing it to you,
The name Tebutinnang.
It is gone, gone, gone—Tebutinnang—o—o!"

and "Gone, gone, gone—Tebutinnang—o—o!" we kept roaring after him until not an atom of the old name could possibly have been left inside the circle and the spirits outside were beyond any reasonable doubt totally preoccupied in devouring it.

The little girl rose to her feet at a sign from her grandfather and, standing in the very centre of our circle, was crowned by him with a fillet of coconut leaf. In the silence that fell upon us then I was called to approach and take her hands in mine.

"What name do you give this girl child?" the old man asked.

"The name of my daughter, Rosemary."

"And you?"—he turned to her— "Is it in your heart to take that name?"

"It is in my heart," she answered clearly, and suddenly all her kinsfolk raised a great shout together:

"Enough! Enough! Let her take the name of Roti-mé-ré!"

Without another word, the old man spilled oil from a coconut shell upon her head and, patting it gently all the time, muttered so low that only she and I could hear his words:

24

"By this crowning with a fillet,
By this anointing with oil,
You have taken a name—
Roti-mé-ré—o—o!
It shall lie safe on you in this place,
The enclosure of the sun and moon.
It shall lie safe on you outside,
For the sun and moon shall be with it—
Roti-mé-ré—o—o!
 Blessings and Peace upon you,
 Blessings and Peace."

I found I had a touch of heat stroke that evening, which naturally pleased my name-child a lot when grandfather told her what it meant. According to him, it only went to show how strong the sun had been for his magic that noontide. And the proof of that was that a bit of coconut leaf on which he had called down the sun's blessing cured me in less than a week by merely staying under my pillow.

2

Rainy Day

My adoption, away back in 1918, into the Tarawa sept of the royal and priestly clan of Karongoa[1] had given me the right to practice the magic of rain-making and rain-dismissing (incidentally also of eclipse-undoing) whenever the fancy took me. Furthermore, my clan fathers had most earnestly coached me in the mysteries of all these useful arts and I, for my part, had just as sedulously tried to get the knack of them, from the moment I became a sun king. But, despite our united goodwill and industry, my exercises in spellbinding had never managed to pull down even one small shower or avert a single unwanted raindrop up to the time in 1922 when Reggie McClure, our new chief arrived at Ocean Island with Dorothy, his beautiful wife. I was therefore not at all surprised when, out of season and against all hope, the day of their arrival turned out wet.

[1] *A Pattern of Islands.*

Methven did explain, as we led them up the streaming hill-side past headquarters office then up again past the central prison yard, the parade ground, the police barracks, that this was the first rain we had had for over six weeks. But the thought of that did not visibly cheer them as we bored, heads down, into the teeth of the downpour, and I had to fall back on my own thoughts for solace.

It was at least sure, I reminded myself, that they would find the residency waterproof. Methven having been, as usual, grossly overloaded with station chores, I had insisted—with a solicitude which had left him strangely ungrateful—on taking personal charge of all the repairs the rickety old building needed. He fancied my ability at that sort of job a lot less than I did myself. But it was a great comfort to me now to have seen every rust-riddled corrugated-iron sheet of the roof replaced before my own eyes by a new one.

A sunburst between heavy clouds cheered us as we topped the rise. The house, two hundred yards away, looked sud-denly enchanted as we approached it along the sodden cricket field's eastern boundary. Set cool in the dappled shadow of palm trees and vivid against the deep dark green of the calo-phyllum forest, its new scarlet roof and ivory-white paint-work shouted a swift gay welcome to us in the golden-wet light.

"Why, what a beautiful bungalow!" exclaimed blue-eyed Mrs. McClure: "I didn't expect anything like this."

"You must have taken a lot of trouble to get it ready for us," added her husband, no less kind than she.

What sheer banalities to be recording after nearly thirty-five years, you may well think! But for Methven and me they were very far from being banal. No such spontaneous graciousness had ever leapt for us, from the saturnine lips of Reggie's predecessor, E. C. Eliot, and this free and easy approach of a chief and his lady to two subordinates was something totally new in our official experience.

We threw each other a covert, half-frightened grin, as if to say, "Marvellous! But careful, now, careful! This may be nothing but eyewash." Nevertheless, I think we were both already sure enough in our hearts that these two were going to be something much nearer to all of us on Ocean Island than the usual senior stuffed shirt and proconsular camisole of our imperial epoch.

The rain came sluicing down again worse than ever as we reached the broad front steps. But the genial spell of that sunny half-minute stayed with us. The weather didn't seem to matter to anyone any longer as Reggie and his Mrs.—or Dolly, as all of us from the outset affectionately called her among ourselves—were taken round their new home.

I noticed with smugness that there wasn't a single leak anywhere in the main building, not even in that tricky corner of the back verandah where the roof over the passageway to the guest-room annexe took off. My new roof had, in fact, most nobly passed the test of its first rainy day. I spoke brightly, on the strength of it, of how Mr. Eliot's orderly had been wont to rush around in wet weather scattering buckets and basins to catch the drips that trickled from the ceilings.

"Well," said Reggie with an amiable laugh, "we're certainly glad you managed to arrange things better for us than that!"

We passed into the guest-room as he was speaking. It was a fine big room with a private verandah and a bathroom of its own. Its appointments were, naturally, not as sumptuous as those which the plutocrat Phosphate Commissioners regarded as proper for occasional visitors (meaning, most probably, themselves) down at Uma, in the palace of their Ocean Island manager. But, for all that, we of the bureaucracy, with our less regal notions of the home comforts due to authority, couldn't help feeling that that extra bathroom at the residency did constitute one of the real highlights of our local civilization. I stepped into it for one last, proud look alone at its shining bronze shower fixture while the others were admiring the verandah.

The shower rose shone as bright as ever. It wasn't this, though, that held me there transfixed, but something on the wall beyond it. A trickle of water. Not a very big trickle— not heavy enough, for example, to run a straight course down the wall. And that, for me, was the meanest thing about it: a small, straight trickle in a corner might possibly have had a chance of passing unnoticed; but nobody could possibly miss this infernal, drunken, dancing dribble that zigzagged so madly across the paintwork from where the wall joined the ceiling up left of the bath's head to the concrete floor down right of its foot. And nobody seeing it could possibly fail to deduce that, somewhere over the bathroom, my egregious new roof must have a leak in it.

I like to believe that at least some of my depression in that moment was due to honest shame for a job incompetently done. But I am bound to confess that the dominant thought in my mind as I stood gaping at the trickle was of the ignominy of being shown up, within an hour of our new chief's arrival, for the ass I had made of myself fiddling with work outside my province. The McClures must not enter the bathroom—they just mustn't be allowed to, I told myself firmly, as I stepped back into the bedroom shutting the door behind me.

They were still on the verandah, but Methven was in the room, looking my way. That made an excellent chance of signalling to him. I did so. Nothing could have been clearer than the way I shook my head at the bathroom, jerked my thumb at the exit doorway and mouthed at him dumbly, "Lead them out—out—out!"

But he chose to regard my desperate facial contortions as a series of ill-timed grimaces pulled at him for no reason but the idiot gaiety of my heart. Sparing nought but a single austere glance in my direction, he strode without pause to the bath-room door and flung it open. A moment later, the McClures came in from the verandah and followed him. While he stayed at the doorway, they went in.

I stood waiting for the ironic laugh that would wither me. "*You silly little boy!*" I heard my headmaster sneering: I wasn't on Ocean Island any longer but back at school, in the Upper Sixth classroom. For some reason or other, that day I was remembering the Lower Sixth had been there too, seated in the front row of desks while the Upper Sixth con-strued Juvenal from the back row; and I had just perpetrated a false quantity. It was a very silly one, I knew; true enough also, I was still undergrown at $17\frac{1}{2}$; but the headmaster himself had seen fit to make a prefect of me, and the savage injustice of that 'silly little boy' of his before an audience like that had left me ever since stupidly quick to resent even the best-deserved sarcasms of my seniors.

But no sound of laughter, no sarcasm, came from the bath-room. It wasn't conceivable that either of them could have failed to see that miserable trickle. But they kept it to themselves. They knew I had seen it and chose to believe—bless them!—that I would have it put right as soon as I could. "Everything is very nice indeed," said Mrs. McClure brightly, coming back into the bedroom, and her husband, following her, added his own kind word or two of thanks. I was their grateful slave from that day on.

Methven's all-seeing eye had of course spotted the leak at once. I waited with resignation for his fatherly comments. But he withheld his fire until the next morning, after breakfast. I was about to leave for the residency when a sergeant of police, smartly saluting, appeared on the verandah and handed me a long, clumsy object of galvanized iron together with a letter. The document ran as follows:

My dear young Sir,

I have the honour to send you herewith, by the hand of Sergeant Nape, one six-foot length of galvanized iron ridge-capping.

This kind of capping, as you may possibly recollect, is used to cover the gap between the two slopes of a roof where they come together at the ridge. Serious leaks are likely to occur in wet weather wherever even only a single length has been omitted —as, for example, over the spare bathroom at the residency.

If you will be good enough to signify your assent to Sergeant Nape, I will cause the omission to be rectified while you are giving our new Chief his first instructions on how to run the Colony to your liking.

I have the honour to be,

My dear young Sir,

Your observant old friend,

(signed) S. C. METHVEN.

PS. Please leave the ridge-capping with Sergeant Nape in any case.

What he didn't ask was that I should let our new chief
know that the leak had been my silly fault, not his.

Fellow Exiles

In addition to a working contingent of seven or eight hundred
labourers from the Gilbert group, the British Phosphate Commissioners used to employ about fifty Chinese artisans and
eight hundred coolies in their mining operations on Ocean
Island. The artisans were a quiet, hardworking class who
thought as proudly of their social status as of their various
crafts, and held themselves aloof from the coolies except to
give them advice or moral support on occasion. The coolies
were a varied, colourful, turbulent crowd signed on in
Hong Kong, and for that reason treated locally as British
subjects, but in fact largely drawn from the slums of
Canton.

The great majority of the coolies, like the mechanics, were
tremendous workers. Though they were on the average small
and pathetically frail-looking, they had the mighty hearts of
their race, and their output of mined phosphate per man-day
was astonishingly higher than that of the husky Gilbertese.
But their number was not without its natural quota of cheerful
leadswingers, and the weekly magistrate's court—over which
the resident commissioner presided—usually dealt with well
over a thousand cases of absenteeism a year.

The contract of indenture explained in Hong Kong to every
recruit before signature contained a penal clause which rendered
him subject to fine or, at his own option, imprisonment for
being absent from his work without leave. The law allowed
the court reasonable latitude for the variation of penalties
according to cases; but, if my memory serves me right, the
formula that Reggie McClure generally used for first offenders
was a fine of a twentieth of a month's basic pay or, alter-
natively, two days' imprisonment for every day of absence.

The same conditions applied to the Gilbertese labourers, but there was very little absenteeism among these.

A good deal of fuss was to be raised some years later about the retention of penal clauses in contracts of employment. But I never could see the force of the objection in relation to the facts at Ocean Island. In signing on to work for a wage there, the recruit, whether Gilbertese or Chinese, committed his employer to the expenses of housing, feeding and doctoring him free of charge as long as he was away from home, also of repatriating him on termination of the agreement. He knew in advance that none of these forms of payment could be withheld from him for any reason whatever, once he was on Ocean Island. His wilful refusal to work after arrival thus amounted to a fraud, against which the contract very rightly tried to protect the wretched employer with a penal clause.

In those days, the majority of habitual absentees among the Chinese welcomed a few days in prison as an alternative to allowing a fine, however small, to be deducted from their month's pay-packet. The exercise of this option gave them a happy sense of scoring all round: nobody got their money, the government had to keep them boarded and lodged, the employer lost their work for the term of the sentence.

But there was one pair of gifted professionals who had things more constructively organized. The speciality of these two was never to check in for work on Saturdays. Week after week they came up on the same charge to the small thatched courthouse under the palms, bowed pleasantly to Reggie on the bench, pleaded guilty, bowed again when sentenced, and, producing a handsome black cash-box, obviously their common property, paid on the nail for their sins. They were good enough to explain to the interpreter one day, in Reggie's private office, why a little thing like a fine meant nothing to them. They had discovered that there was money in cooked food. Their Saturdays were spent, not in unproductive idleness but in preparing delicious cakes and baked meats for sale, over the weekend, to their fellow workers. According to the interpreter,

33

who was all on their side, the loss of their day's industry to the employer was repaid a thousand times over by the happiness and strength that coolies and mechanics alike derived from their superb cooking. It looked to Reggie and me as if he might have been right when, the next Saturday night, we walked through the brightly lit hurly-burly of the Chinese location and saw the milling, eager, laughing crowd that surged around their stall, hard by the recreation hall where the mah jong and fantan schools held session. And, as Reggie said, it became a pleasure to extract the maximum fines from them after that, seeing how stuffed with £1 notes that cash-box had looked, open between them on the counter. I couldn't help feeling, though, that the B.P.C. manager had some right on his side when he got us to cancel their contracts and shipped them, still cheerfully smiling, back to Hong Kong.

Droughts and Caverns

When the rains were regular on Baanaba, no habitation of man could have been more beautifully bowered than ours in the dark green of forests, the starry white of lilies, the flung foam of scarlet and crimson petals. But every seven or eight years there came a drought, and things were different then. There were no more flowers anywhere after two rainless months. After six, the pawpaws and guavas, the custard apples and soursops were dead, the mangoes and wild almonds dying. After twelve, half of the island's coconut palms stood headless, while those that lived on, their leaves burned rusty black, had been fruitless for many weeks. Then, even the mighty, deep-rooted forest of calophyllum trees that covered the island's middle was stripped of its leaves. Our two thousand acres of phosphate and coral rock, left naked to the sun-glare, lay flinging back the savage heat in a white-hot column to heaven.

That soaring shaft of refraction stood like a pitiless sentinel on guard over the land. It was the barrier against which the rainclouds beat and were divided. When the westerly monsoon was due to begin, you could stand on the south-west point of the land and watch the black battalions riding up the sky towards you, trailing an unbroken curtain of rain across the sea's face below them. "At last!" you would say to yourself, "It's coming. It must be coming this time," and, as if to mock your hope, it would come so near you could hear the swish and whisper of it on the water. If you looked up then you could see the cloud's edge sweep almost to the zenith. Almost, yet not near enough: in the last moment, you saw it waver, halt in the middle, torn apart there by the uprushing column of furnace-hot air. You watched its sundered halves pass by, spilling their torrents into the sea a few hundred yards from the coast on either hand, while, between them, under a sullen grey but rainless sky, the stricken land thirsted on.

The Gilbert Islands to eastwards had their droughts as well— still have them, doubtless—but they are atolls, not upthrust rocks like Baanaba, and in an atoll one can always have water drinkable enough, for all its brackish taste, from any seepage well. That same water also, held twelve feet under the sand in pans of the coral table on which every atoll stands, is nearly always fresh enough to keep most of the coconut trees bearing some few nuts, even through the worst of droughts.

The Baanabans of old had no such help from sea and soil for their food trees; nevertheless, they did command certain underground reserves of drinking water, for the coral core of their island was as riddled with hidden grottoes and galleries as a Stilton cheese with the burrowings of *animalculae*.

Aeons ago, the coral had grown plateau-wise on a submarine mountain-top very near the surface of the sea. When it broke surface, countless seabirds, for countless centuries, made it their home and its three square miles were piled high with a bed of guano sixty feet deep in the middle. Then the mountain sank into the depths until, millions of years later, another convulsion of the sea's bed flung its top towering again, this time three hundred feet clear above the waves. In the throes of that upheaval, the coral plateau under its load of guano (now sea-changed into phosphate of lime) was twisted, flawed, splintered, rent asunder a thousand ways. So were born the wonderful *bangabanga*, or caverns, of Baanaba.

The *bangabanga* stretched mile-long, an uncounted series of chambers and corridors, chimneys and passages, through the eastern half of the island, here rising to the light of day, there twisting amid festooned tree-roots through the middle depths, and again plunging deep through the bowels of the rock to the edge of echoing abysses. Wherever the rain, soaking through topsoil and phosphate into this dark labyrinth, could find a pan or a pocket to lie in, there it accumulated trickle by trickle through seasons of plenty, untouched until the hour of need. The entrances to the scores of branching passages where no pools could collect had been blocked in the course of generations with heavy boulders, so that no one living had ever explored the endless ramifications of the system beyond the three or four quarter-mile chains of grottoes where the women went water-gathering.

Grim stories were told of girls who had ventured off the beaten track into the black unknown, never to be seen again. Some said that these were only inventions, meant to warn the young against too much curiosity. I always thought myself that the known passageways were daunting enough in themselves to forbid wandering, the roofs of their principal chambers, sooted with the torches of sixty dead generations, less than head-high, the tunnels between them no more than burrows through which the only way for a woman of ordinary size to squirm was on her back, clawing at the rock above her face. Yet, such is the sanifying force of usage backed by the pressure of a genuine need that women who, for fear of a thousand clutching ghosts, would never have ventured, even in twos or threes, through the quiet glimmer of a starlit night, would plunge alone as a matter of course into the murk of those sinister abysses without even a match to guide their groping hands and feet.

But no such solo performances were allowed when a drought had lasted for more than four quarters of the moon. Then, in olden times, it was death for anyone to be found loitering alone anywhere near a *bangabanga*: the women did their water-getting all together, at dictated times, each with her strict allowance of coconut shells to fill and carrying a lighted torch, so that her companions could observe her every movement. Precautions of this kind, rigidly enforced before the days of British rule by councils of old men representing all the four Baanaban villages, might suffice to eke out the cave supply for as long as two years. But that was the limit. If the drought lasted longer, the only possible source of supply left was in the rainfall at sea.

Men would go out every day in their canoes hunting for showers, with catchments of sun-shrivelled coconut fronds set up so that their butt ends rested in wooden bowls, into which they were intended to conduct the rain. Their wives and children would go with them to revel in the divine wetness and drink it in through every pore. In that way, they could do without the precious collected drops and store these up in coconut shells for the aged or infirm who stayed ashore.

Every coconut palm over ten years old on Ocean Island carried the record of at least one drought upon it. A dry spell of no more than four or five months would start a constriction of the trunk at the neck where the first fronds sprouted. After that, you could see the tree being slowly strangled as it

37

stood. But up to the very last moment before the head was utterly withered away, its life could be saved by rain. If that happened, no matter how far it was gone on the way to death, it would be bearing nuts once more within the next nine months, its wind-tossed head as richly green as ever, its stem grown full and sappy again up where the new fronds sprang. Only, just below the new growth, that constriction of the trunk would remain to show where the drought had clutched it.

You could count six such corsettings in the stems of the oldest trees. That carried you back forty years or so—about two-thirds of a coconut's natural span. The record could go no further than that into the past, because the seventh drought back from 1924, which happened in the middle eighteen-seventies, wiped out every palm in the island. Indeed, it destroyed every plant of any kind except the salt bush and ironwood scrub by the sea and the deep forest of calophyllum trees on the crest of the island. The forest survived because it had its roots far down in hidden caves and galleries where the Baanabans, had they but known the way, would have found water in plenty for their need. But that source of supply was discovered only half a century later when there was no longer any use for it. By then, the mining operations which revealed the caves were paying the islanders royalties enough to build fine village reservoirs and, in addition, accumulate a fund that, in the years to come, would enable them to buy a greener, kinder home of their own choosing, far from the droughts of the doldrums.

The Curse of Nakaa

An uneasy silence would fall upon the older villagers whenever one mentioned the great drought of the eighteen-seventies. I often got the impression that some shared dread constrained them never to talk of it. It was not until 1930, when I had known them for sixteen years, that anyone told me of the horrors it had meant for them. It was old Eri, the native magistrate of Baanaba, who spoke of it then. Not that he had visited me expressly to do so, but his story sprang naturally from a pathetic request he had been deputed to make on behalf of the older villagers.

The British Phosphate Commissioners had recently asked for a hundred-acre extension of their diggings, and a party of young men was heckling the council of elders about the price to be demanded for the concession. Eri came to me deeply disturbed. "Nobody will want to pay the young men's price for our dust," he put it, "and that will be the end of our hope of buying a better home than this for our grandchildren to inherit. So, in the end, the curse of Nakaa will rest upon their heads also."

"The curse of Nakaa?" I echoed blankly—"What *are* you talking about, Eri?"

"About the great drought," he said, and that launched him on his story.

"I was a young man then, and my parents, who lived in Uma village, had arranged for me to take a wife from Buakoni-kai. She was a girl named Marawa, very beautiful in my eyes, and we were to be married at the full of the fourth moon at the season of the Pleiades. But when the third moon went out, and for three months no rain had fallen, her father said to mine, 'You will need your son to fish for you and we shall need Marawa to fetch water for us now that a drought has set in.' And my father answered, 'Even so. Let there be no marriage until the rains return.'

"Our hearts were sore at that and my mother tried to comfort us, saying, 'Patience. The drought will soon end.' But it did not end; and even when the sun showed a full year gone we knew that it would not break yet, for the rainclouds at sea, from which we had contrived to collect water up to then, ceased to come near us. Then our council of elders issued an edict:

40

'From now on, let no household take more than one coconut shell of water a day from the *bangabanga*.'

"So the water was made to last for another whole year. But long before the next solstice in the south our food trees were gone; not one stood living in the land. We had nothing but fish to eat, and the fish often stayed so far from our shores, that for many days together there was none to be caught anywhere. We were already half starved when the drought sickness came, that white men call beriberi.

"People's gums rotted in their mouths; their teeth fell out; their bodies were covered in ulcers. They fell in the pathways and died there; and where they died their bodies remained, for who was strong enough to carry corpses home for burial rites? So the curse of Nakaa rested on the land."

It was strange to hear a man like Eri, stern old pillar of the Protestant Mission that he was, talk of the curse of a pagan god as if he believed in it. Nakaa, so the ancient myth had it, was the all-seeing guardian of the gate between the worlds of the living and the dead, who, in the beginning of time, had decreed eternal torture by impalement in his pit for those who neglected the funeral rites of their own kin.

"But Eri," I protested, "a Christian like you can't fear Nakaa or his curses any longer."

"Nakaa is a spirit of darkness," he answered earnestly. "Shall any man do away with him by becoming a Christian? And how shall we forget our unburied dead? These walk like ghosts in our hearts for ever." And then, after a long silence: "In the middle of the third year, when the waterholes were nearly dry, word came from Buakonikai that Marawa's parents had died. Things were a little better for us in Uma than in Buakonikai; Uma is by the sea; we had found seaweed to suck, and some said that this protected us against the sickness. But we were very weak. I was the only one of our house who could walk a hundred paces. So my mother said to me, 'Go now to Buakonikai. Speak to the brother of

Marawa's father and, if he will let her go, bring her to us here. So, from this drought you shall have a wife and I a daughter.'

"At her words, the strength came back to my legs. I made nothing of the long walk to Buakonikai. I came to the house of Marawa's father's brother. My heart said to me, 'Now you will see her.' But alas! when I lifted the screen to enter, she was not there. Only her father's brother was within, and he was dead. And the stink of corruption was everywhere around me as I walked through the village to her father's house.

"I found her with her parents. She had laid their bodies side by side and herself at their feet. The sickness was heavy upon her. Her lips were black and her body eaten with ulcers. But she was still beautiful for me. I think she had been asleep before I entered; but when I lifted the screen she awoke and smiled at me, saying, 'I knew I should see you again,' and tried to sit up, but fell back looking into my eyes as I sat down beside her. Lying there, she smiled again and sighed very slow and deep. The smile stayed on her lips. She was dead.

"I laid her beside her mother, her feet towards the west. I lifted her head from behind between my hands and looked down into her eyes. So, bending over her, I whispered the spell called The Lifting of the Head, to make her way straight into the land of our ancestors."

He paused a long while, remembering. I did not presume to ask him then what magic words he had whispered over his dead love; but, months later, he gave them to me of his own accord, and this is how they ran:

> I lift your head, I straighten your way, for you are going
>   home, Marawa, Marawa,
> Home to Innang and Mwaiku, Roro and Bouru,
> You will pass over the sea of Manra in your canoe with
>   pandanus fruit for food;
> You will find harbour under the lee of Matang and Atiia
>   and Abaiti in the West,

Even the homes of your ancestors.

Return not to your body; leave it never to return, for you
    are going home, Marawa, Marawa.

And so, Farewell for a moon or two, a season or two.

Farewell! your way is straight; you shall not be led
    astray.

Blessings and peace go with you. Blessings and peace.

"So I brought no daughter to my mother," the old man
said, suddenly coming out of his silence. "Time went on.
The waterholes were dry, but the rainclouds at sea had returned. Also, we of Uma village went down to the reef at
low tide and lay covered with mats in shallow pools, so that
our skins drank in the wetness.

"And on a day, I took my mother with me to a pool under
the lee of certain rocks. We lay there, our heads resting on
wooden pillows which I had brought, and soon we fell
asleep.

"I did not wake until the rising tide floated the pillow from
under me, so that my head was spilled into the water. That
nearly drowned me, but at last I was able to kneel, and then I
remembered my mother. She was not beside me. I looked
out to sea; she was not there. I turned my eyes to the beach;
she was floating there, on the edge of the tide. She had
drowned beside me as I slept. How many times had she
called me, and I deaf to her cries?

"A ship arrived not long after . . . a trading ship from New
Zealand. The captain took my father and me, with most of
the others who remained alive, to the island of Oahu, near
Honolulu. There we lived until my father died, six years
later, and then I returned to this place, because I owned no
land anywhere else. Others returned with me, but none of
us had ever been happy here. And since the Kambana [Com-
pany] came and began to pay us for our dust, we have hoped
that, one day, it may buy all the rest together for a great
price. With that money, the government could buy a happier

43

home for our children's children to dwell in. Help us in this, we beg you."

He sat in silence a full minute staring over my shoulder into the past. Then he rose. "A home for our children's children not haunted by the ghosts of our unburied dead," he whispered, more to himself than to me, and left without another word.

3

Final Lesson

Reggie McClure had had about enough of me at headquarters by late August, 1922, so it was decided that I should now go across to the Gilbert Islands and get along with the business of starting a lands commission there. The date of my proposed departure had been fixed, and all farewell calls save one religiously paid, when news came through that my ship was going to arrive the next morning, exactly a week earlier than expected.

That same day, my name-child Roti-mé-ré came to give me one last lesson in Gilbertese manners, which means that she wasn't visiting me under the name of Roti-mé-ré at all, but under her educational alias of Female Straighten-ways, and it was as Straighten-ways that I greeted her.

My invariable response to these cultural calls of hers had hitherto been to drop in at her grandfather's house bearing small gifts some days later. Three days was the minimum delay prescribed by custom; but it was clear I couldn't live up to the time protocols on this occasion; and I hoped that, in the circumstances, she might waive the strict formalities and accept my gift—a modest ten-shilling note—as she was leaving me.

She gave the note a long, shining look as it lay across her palm—this was the first time I had ever given her money. "What a great sum it is!" she murmured at last: "I have never before held so much in my hand to squander according to my heart."

And then, almost in the same breath, her face suddenly tragic, she cried aloud, "But, alas, I cannot take it! It would not be correct."

I thought she was afraid her grandmother might scold her for taking money from me instead of gifts in kind. "I shouldn't worry about that if I were you," I said with idiot indulgence, closing her fingers on the note: "The new things you have told me today are worth much more than this. Take it with my thanks, and now be off with you."

She threw up an arm as if I had struck her. "No!" she breathed, and again, "No! Those things were my love-gift to you. I cannot take money for them." Pressing the note back into my hand, she turned and walked quickly out of the house. She was half-way down the garden path before I could stop her.

When she consented to be seated again she left me in no doubt as to the clumsiness of my offence against her people's philosophy of giving and receiving. If a friend brought you a present, you couldn't go offering him instant payment for it as if he had come without love, like a trader, with something to sell you. The only proper procedure was to sit thinking of nothing but his loving-kindness first of all. You thought of it continuously for three days at least. Only then you visited him with an answering gift, and not even then with any idea of settling an account with him, but simply because you wanted him to know that your love went out to meet his, fullness for fullness.

"So you think this will have to wait," I was driven to say at last, holding up the note, "until something or other brings me back to Baanaba?"

"I think it would be correct for you to hold it until you next visit our house," was her forlorn answer. Her heartbroken gaze dwelt on it awhile. "Alas!" Then she added anxiously, "You won't forget, will you?"

"Of course not, you silly. Haven't you just been telling me the right way to remember? But instead of sitting and thinking of your kindness for just three or four days, I shall be doing so for three or four months. I shall like that."

"And I shall be happy waiting for your return," she ended, getting up and tearing herself away: "Alas!"

Her back view as I watched her disappear round a bend of the path was the saddest view I have ever had of anyone.

I was just sitting down, rather depressed, to think what more I could do about it when I heard a sudden scream from afar and looked up to see her rushing back along the path, her whole person radiating happiness.

"Why, welcome again, Straighten-ways," I called as she came bouncing up the steps, "and what is it now?"

"Not Straighten-ways," she laughed, standing with dramatically outflung arms before me: "That woman Straighten-ways has just left you. Behold now your name-child, Roti-mé-ré!"

All by herself she had found the way through—how, in short, to set one custom to cancel out another. As Straighten-ways she was helplessly bound by obedience to the immemorial

47

usage she professed to be teaching me; but as my name-child, usage itself ordained that her first obligation of obedience was owed personally to me. She took the note gently from my hand.

"Do you order me to take this gift, Kurimbo?"

"I order you, Roti-mé-ré, name-sister of my daughter."

"I obey, Kurimbo," she called: "The kind one, you!" and, bidding me good-bye, ran off, the note pressed to her happy heart.

Way to the World's Edge

The lovely farewell to his dead sweetheart that old Eri gave me is only a scrap from a mass of evidence that one branch at least of the Gilbertese ancestors migrated into the central Pacific from far western lands. The seven western Paradises named in the old man's prayer—Innang and Matang, Bouru and Mwaiku, Abaiti, Roro, Atiia (of which the last three are Maori paradises also)—are called *rikia* in the Gilbertese version. Though I have rendered this word broadly 'home' in the translation, the basic meaning of growth or origin contained in the root *riki* perhaps makes 'fatherland' the more precise interpretation.

But most of that first stream from the West which planted colonies in the equatorial islands passed on, a mighty horde, pressing southward through the sixteen Gilbert atolls, through the eight Ellices, past lonely Rotuma, across the empty vastitude beyond it, until they came to Savai'i and Upolu of Samoa. There they and their descendants won a foothold and stayed for perhaps a thousand years, too far removed from the *rikia* of their forefathers to be harking back to them except (in the rituals of the dead) as 'ghost lands.' But their kinsmen on the equator were nearer by a thousand miles to the ancient cradles of their race, and had no such rich new homes as Savai'i or Upolu to hold them settled within their own borders. There was constant traffic and at least some inter-marriage between these and the lands back west along the old migration route.

Matairongo and Kabintongo, Baantongo and Waituru, Tanabai and Bikaara, Nabanaba and Onouna, Baree and Tab-euna, Ruanuna and Kiroro are a round dozen out of the scores of magically named places called 'the home of the Breed of Kiroro'—the 'line of ghost lands stretching westwards as far as the very homes of the dead in the sea of Manra,' as the ancient travel stories used to describe them—with which the early

49

colonists of the Gilbert atolls habitually exchanged friendship and warfare, dancing parties and wives.

The genealogies tell of marriages and feasts arranged up to about thirty generations ago between kings of Tarawa, for example, and king's daughters of Onouna, Ruanuna and Kiroro. But then came the re-invasion of the Gilberts from Samoa. Between twenty-five and thirty generations back, the islands were overwhelmed by wave upon wave of the kins-men whose forefathers, a thousand years earlier, had passed southwards to Savai'i and Upolu.

From the time of that invasion onwards, no more tales of East-West alliances, or even visits, appear in the family histories. It is easy to see why. For the invaders, a millenium of history in Samoa had established that country instead of some remote western paradise as the *Buto*, or navel, or centre of the populated world and first of created lands. Since the newcomers came to the Gilberts as conquerors, it was naturally back to Samoa and not to the West that their descendants in the Gilberts counted their human generations and turned for their knowledge of human geography. Ancestors of their van-quished cousins like the old kings of Tarawa, no longer socially important, became a *bu-n-anti*, a 'breed of ghosts,' and the western lands with which these had trafficked so spaci-ously came, in the course of time, to be treated in song and story only as 'ghost lands' like the ancestral paradises themselves, never to be reached by living men except in dreams.

Once the ghost world closed down in men's minds upon the West, the thought of falling too far to leeward of his islands in the S.E. trades became loaded for every Gilbertese mariner with a double horror. If he failed in his attempts to beat to landward against the mighty winds and sweeping swells of the navigating season (March to September), he was not simply a man forced to turn and run before the gale for a last desperate chance of safety beyond unknown horizons, but one already doomed to pass through dreadful fears to a yet more dreadful end in the abyss at the world's western edge.

So as not to stray outside the limits—especially the westward limit—of safety when they navigated beyond sight of land, generations of fishermen and voyagers built up out of their experience a system of *betia*, or seamarks, by which, if only a man knew enough of them, he could be sure of his position in relation to any island of the Gilbert group. These signposts in mid-ocean might be shoals of fish, flocks of birds, masses of floating weed, or merely the way certain fish, or birds, or weeds behaved. They could be shapes of waves, or their size, or direction, or frequencies; they could be lines of driftwood, or shining streaks on the face of the waters, or conditions of atmosphere, like high or low visibility, or even the smell of the air, ranging from land scents to *te boi-n-anti*, the 'stink-of-ghosts,' that told you how near you were drifting to the western point of no return. Impalpable for the most part to any average European, these *betia* were as clear and significant to the ordinary Gilbertese fisherman as a bent blade of grass or the displacement of a twig underfoot might be to a tracker of the Australian bush.

The point of no return in the western seas was a *betia* called the Fishtrap of Kabaki, a scattered line of leaves and driftwood, said to stretch in the navigating season from the ghost lands in the far North-West south-eastwards to the latitude of Samoa. This line was the threshold of horror where the lost mariner first smelt the stink of ghosts. Beyond, the sea began to slope down like a river, its swift stream bearing him resistlessly westwards into a region of dead calms, where thronging voices whispered around him, "You are lost! You are lost!" and the monstrous *uu*-fish waited to suck him down. And if he escaped the *uu*-fish, the sea, ever more steeply sloping, swept him on into the zone of wildfire, where a man had two shadows —one on the sail, one on the water—and green bubbles of light burst upwards from the depths to dance about his head, while the voices of women screamed for fear of a clutching Thing he knew to be very near but could not see. And if the Thing let him pass, then, for a day and a night, he was whirled through a zone called *te-uabuki-te-re*, 'the-capsize-the-somersault,' where the ocean gathered itself in a last enormous race towards the lip of the world, and in the dreadful silence only the thin voice of a single bird was heard, wailing, "I kaawa . . . I kaawa . . . I kaawa! (I am unhappy . . . unhappy . . . unhappy!)" until the plunging waters flung him out with his canoe, over and over, down, down, down into the black and bellowing abyss of Mone.

Sleepy Navigator

I eventually got my lands commission started at Butaritari, up in the northern Gilberts. But while waiting at Tarawa for a ship to take me there I took a run down to Maiana, the next island to southward.

It was stupid to risk that particular crossing in a sailing boat without auxiliary power. Although the gut between the southern tip of Tarawa and the northern tip of Maiana is under twenty miles wide, it is a forever shifting welter of currents that sweep crisscross over and under each other from ocean to ocean. Once the land astern is out of sight (and, from a boat, you lose the tree-tops of an ordinary atoll at less than eight miles off shore) an engineless craft caught in the wrong stream can be whipped eight miles to leeward of its course before those on board begin to think of looking for the tree-tops ahead; and by the time they have realized that nothing but a thousand leagues of empty ocean lie before them, another five miles of leeway will have been lost. Failing some miraculous change of wind or current then, not a man of them will ever see land again.

But we were lucky that day. When we raised the north end of Maiana we found we had been set a few miles to east-ward of it. Some eddy, in fact, had swept us not to leeward at all, but upwind, and the rest of the trip was a quick run downwind to anchor under the lee of the lagoon reef.

It was only when, some days later, I sat talking to old Kimaere the navigator in his canoe-shed by the weather beach that I heard how easily things might have been different. According to him, only a pack of fools who hadn't a notion of how to look at the sea would have chanced the crossing the day we had.

"But we got here perfectly safe, Kimaere," I protested.

"You got here on *te aira-n-anti* (a ghost current)," he replied cuttingly, meaning that our eddy had been nothing but one of ten million tricks the sea was forever playing in those twisted waters and never repeating.

"Very well, we had the luck of fools, which can't be expected twice," I said: "so, now that you've got me nicely frightened, please tell me what I'm to do about getting back to Tarawa tomorrow."

"Tomorrow, Kurimbo?" The old man swept a hand dramatically seaward—"Look at it! Tomorrow? You can't mean what you are saying."

The sea looked perfect to me. A moderate surf on the reef's edge told of swells not too towering in the vast blue-black expanse beyond it. The great dome of the sky was

sparkling clear. A smart, steady twenty-knot wind was blowing from the south-east. There couldn't have been more
promising conditions for the homeward run, by my reckoning, and I said so.

"But look at it, Kurimbo . . . *listen* to it!"

His voice was so full of shocked reproof, I simply had to
make an effort to see and hear what he meant. It seemed that
what he wanted me to see was something significant about the
angle at which the breakers were charging the reef; and what
he wanted me to hear was a kind of low screaming note behind
the mild roar of tumbling waters—*tangi-n te aira* (the cry of the
current), he called it. All that was children's stuff, according to
him. But, despite his careful directions and repetitions, my
dull eyes and sluggish ears totally failed to register. It soon
became clear he found it hard to put up with so crass a pupil.
He forgave me, though, when at last I offered him a fee to
pilot us home and left the fixing of our sailing date entirely to
him.

It wasn't until nearly five in the afternoon four days later
that he came and reported all currents fair for a getaway. I
went with him to inspect the sea and, while he explained how
dead right the look and sound of it were, I stood wondering
how a five-ton cutter was going to stand up to it: a tremendous surf was crashing on the reef and the wind was blowing
half a gale. However, you can't appoint an expert one
minute and go summarily rejecting his advice the next (not
outside the Colonial Office, anyhow), so I said unwillingly at
last, "All right. Sunset's on us now, though. We'll start at
dawn tomorrow."

But that wasn't soon enough for him; the currents, in his
opinion, were due for a complete change three hours after
sunrise next morning. As the thirty-odd miles we had to sail
from anchorage to anchorage would take us, say, seven hours
in that wind, our safest plan would be to start not later than
twelve o'clock that night, he insisted.

We got away at 11.30, an hour before moonset, under a

double-reefed mainsail and a single jib. Even so, the cutter staggered a lot too much for my liking when the big gusts hit her. But the old man stood easily balancing himself in the bows as he conned her west and north past the reefs we had to skirt before the way to Tarawa lay open. He didn't seem to need any handhold even when we came lurching out from under the lee of the land into the dizzy heave of a monstrous westward-running swell.

A compass was another of the things he could do without. He had his guiding stars for every night of the year and every state of wind or current, he said, and these, with his sense of smell, made him independent of white men's inventions. The only thing he did say he needed, after telling us to steer what my portable compass called E.N.E., was a bit of shut-eye. Yes, just as the moon set and my thirst for his moral support reached its most feverish pitch, he left me sitting in the madly plunging bows and, crawling into a coffin-shaped shelter called the pilot's dog-box on the foredeck, went quietly to sleep.

To be sure, in most kinds of bad weather, a small craft is generally safer riding the enormous surges of the equatorial Pacific than caught in the cruel, short, smashing seas of an angry lagoon. Nevertheless, a really big ocean swell with a high wind right behind it does hold certain dangers peculiar to itself. In the valley ahead of each towering crest there is a windless space where the driven water boils up in directionless pyramids around you, and your small boat, her sails empty and thrashing, can easily wallow herself under. And when the rushing mountain swings her reeling from the depths up, up into the giddy heights, there the full fury of the gale suddenly slams her, and you will have her capsized in a second unless you have thought in advance to ease her up for the blow.

I can't say that my capacity to bear these shocks in silence was improved by the howling blackness of the night. Hardly a guiding star was to be seen for the racing clouds. I had a gnawing conviction, too, that our course had far too much east in it. What with this and that, I have to admit that I succumbed after about an hour and a half to a wild wish to hear the old man's voice again. I went and woke him up.

"What do your stars say now, Kimaere?" I asked him.

He poked his head out of the dog-box and, after sniffing at the air for a few seconds without even a glance at the sky, told me we were only just through the worst of the tide-race round the north end of Maiana.

"Keep her heading always well to the east," he reiterated, as if he had divined the nervous question trembling behind my teeth, and, adding a firm intimation that he would prefer to wake up all on his own the next time, withdrew his head like a snail's into its carapace and went to sleep again.

I stayed in the well-deck aft most of the night, sharing tricks at the helm with the boat captain. A hurricane lamp slung low on a shroud to windward threw a flickering light over the foredeck. It wasn't very bright, but it kept the dog-box well in view from where I sat waiting and watching for the old man to emerge. "Surely he'll be taking another look round *now*," I kept saying to myself as hour after mortal hour ticked by; but never a sign gave he.

At four o'clock I crawled forward and put an ear to the entrance of his shelter. I couldn't believe he intended to pilot us the whole way, on a night like that, in his sleep. There he lay, though, breathing as deep and placid as a fed baby in the cosy darkness, and there he stayed for another eighty minutes without a move. It wanted less than half an hour of sunrise when he suddenly awoke, clawed his way aft and took the tiller from my hand.

"There is Te Rawa-ni-Bairiki straight ahead," he told me, pointing over the bows as if everything was visible through the night. "Now drop the peak. We will jib sail then and run downwind to Betio."

Te Rawa-ni-Bairiki is a tidal passage, connecting lagoon

and ocean, that cuts through the ribbon of Tarawa's main-
land about three miles to eastward of its south-western
tip.

But I was full of mistrust. "You sleep all night, then come
and say, 'There's Bairiki passage ahead!'" I exclaimed.
"How can you possibly pretend to know that for sure? Did a
ghost tell you?"

"Not a ghost, Kurimbo . . . only the smell." It was too
dark to see his face, but I heard a smile in his voice.

"What . . . the smell of Tarawa? Impossible. It's downwind from here."

"Not the land-smell . . . the sea-smell," he corrected me
gently. "That was the voice that said to me as I slept, 'Wake
up!' And then, when I was awake, there was the pull of the
waves."

According to him, the alarm-clock smell he talked of was
peculiar to the sea along the whole length of Tarawa's south
coast: no fisherman worth the name could possibly miss it.
And the pull of the waves, it seemed, was a kind of jerk or
twist or impulse or something that the state of the current
imparted to a craft from its keel upwards. This pull was a
much more localized affair than the smell, I gathered. If we
had been farther to eastward—opposite the Eita passage, for
example—the feel of it would have been quite different. He
tried to make me understand what the feel of the Bairiki one
was actually like: "As it were, a hand plucking at the keel
from below the forefoot," he said of it. But it was no good: I
was half asleep after the night's vigil, and what was awake of
me felt only the wild yawing of the boat as the racing mountain-
tops chased her, and all I had inside me was a desperate longing
for the sunrise. And on that thought I was of a sudden wholly
asleep, slumped there by the tiller.

"Look!" said the old man touching my shoulder a quarter
of an hour later. I woke to find day breaking. The sun was not
yet up, but in the east, the whole firmament from horizon to
zenith was a single translucent flame of daffodil yellow that

E

merged overhead into another flame of unbelievably tender green. But it wasn't the wonder of the dawnlight that he wanted me to admire. "What did I tell you!" he said, pointing north over the wine-dark waters; and there was the purple line of Tarawa's palms, with Bairiki passage two miles away under our lee counter as we went scudding down the coast to Betio and safety.

The Boat that Came Home

The cutter I used for the Maiana trip was the pride of Betio station and the delight of every district officer posted to Tarawa. She had had a strange history up to that time, and was destined years later (if you believe in such a thing as destiny) to find as strange an end. Her story had begun for me personally one day in 1916 when, as a very green district officer, I had sailed eighteen miles across-lagoon to talk to Mrs. Grant about nothing but the renewal of her trade-store licence up at Tarawa North End. The grim old widow was strictly agin the government and had never before honoured me with anything like a confidence; so I really can't guess what led her to treat me all of a sudden to the stuff she spilled about David Kanoa and his home-finding boats.

David Kanoa was the big, gentle Hawaiian half-caste whom she and her late husband, Peter Grant, had befriended in the wild years before the British flag came to the Gilberts. She had found him one morning at sunrise, she said, senseless and bloody on the beach of their trade-store, dumped there out of a barquentine bound from Ponape to Manihiki. "The dirty cows never came back," was all she cared to add to this little bit of pre-history: "so we had him on our hands, see. But me an' me hubby didn't lose nothing on him. He turned out to be a number-one boat-builder. He built us a cutter for nothing but his keep with the lumber we give him. Over thirty years back, that was, but she's still a beaut. Look at her!"

The boat lay moored at the lagoon embayment of a tidal passage from the ocean that cut the narrow land there. From the verandah of the Grant shanty she certainly made a lovely picture, poised like a still, white swan on the emerald flame of the outflowing tide. It wasn't her beauty, though, but her utility that wrung me with desire at the moment. I longed to have just such a craft at my call for regular visits to other islands. Top authority, however, as bone-headed as usual, had recently trodden upon me hard for daring to entertain so expensive a notion.

I was just on the unwise point of telling Mrs. Grant all about it when a swirl of the falling tide made the cutter dance and tug at her moorings. "Look at her!" said the old woman again, "She's trying to get home, she is!"

The strangeness of her phrase snapped me out of my near indiscretion: "Home?" I echoed blankly.

"Well, she was born in along there, ye might say," she replied, and that set her tongue really clacking.

The fact was, she explained, David Kanoa had had his boat-yard by the tidal passage. Not on the lagoon beach, though. No, he had located it carefully a furlong inshore, midway between lagoon and ocean, where the ebb and flow of waters drove through the thickest of the palm grove. It was a fixed idea of his that a boat mustn't on any account be born in sight of the sea. If she was, he always said, she'd never be a land-finder. You couldn't tell then when she might sink with you, miles from any shore. But build her at a place like he had chosen, looking at trees and landlocked water, and she'd remember it in her bones for ever. "Ay," said Mrs. Grant, "and she'd always come back to it, so he claimed. Even without a rudder she'd come safe back to where she'd been born, any of his boats would."

I didn't bother to enquire if she herself believed such ridiculous nonsense: it was too clear she did; also, she was doggedly launched on a long recital of the boats David had built there. But I did manage to ask her at last if any of the craft 'born'—

to use her own word—in the Kanoa yard had ever, to her knowledge, shown the least proof of possessing that peculiar homing instinct she'd mentioned.

It baled her up, but only for a moment. She eyed me distastefully, then barked, "You wouldn't understand, young man. You ain't no kind of a sailor," and, as if I hadn't interruped, went on describing the last craft David had built on Tarawa—a 32-foot cruiser, cutter-rigged, with a fine hold under hatches amidships and a couple of bunks below decks aft. A real ocean-going job; her stem and sternpost, keel and ribs, of local hardwoods; her hull carved-built of two-inch planks from one of those ready-dressed 60-foot pine masts from California that the winds and currents now and then tossed up on the weather beaches of the Gilberts.

Mrs. Grant made a big thing of that pine mast. What tickled her most about it was the secret way it had arrived, with the clear-as-mud intention, she reckoned, of preventing the ruddy government (several years in the saddle by then) from grabbing it for a flagstaff. Instead of rolling itself up on the foreshore like all the rest of its kind, for everyone to see, it had deliberately shot the reef, point first, one night at flood tide, then dived straight into the very tidal passage where the Grants lived, and obligingly come to rest at the bend of the stream by David Kanoa's boat-yard. He and Peter Grant got it sawn into 20-foot lengths, levered ashore and covered up with palm leaves before another soul saw it. Turning it into planks at his leisure then, David had that last boat of his finished within the next two years or so.

"Well, I bet that was the home-findingest of all the craft he ever launched," I got in. "Just fancy! even the timber she was going to be built of coming barging in on its own like that, all the way from California!" To tell the truth, I was bored stiff with that 'ruddy government' line of hers: she was always shooting it, and I'd have liked to get some change out of her if I could; but all she replied to the gibe was, "That's just what I thought meself," and then, after a long pause, "I kinda feel she *will* come back one o' these days, though David's dead an' gone."

"Well, that'll be wonderful!" I told her heavily. "She's the very thing I want—so long as she doesn't cost the government a blanky bean." But she knew as well as I did what nonsense she was talking. David had taken his boat off to Jaluit, in the Marshall Islands, round about 1902. The go-ahead German administration up there was offering fine jobs to craftsmen like him in those days, and he had walked straight into one as soon as he stepped ashore. But dysentery had killed him soon, poor soul, and his masterpiece had been sold at auction to a local German trader.

So there she had been in 1914, away up in Jaluit lagoon, four hundred-odd miles from home, when the Japanese navy came along and occupied the Marshall group. Everyone knew what had happened then. The Japanese had taken the whole bunch of Jaluit traders' boats out to sea, blown the bows out of them with time-charges of guncotton, and left them to founder. There wasn't the ghost of a reason why David's creation should have escaped the fate of the rest, I reminded the old woman, but she only insisted stubbornly, "She'll come back. I kinda feel it."

Too absurd for words, I thought as I left her. What I can't add, however, is that the passage of time showed her 'feeling' up for the silliness it was. It did nothing of the sort. David Kanoa's boat did, in fact, find her way home. Yes, entirely on her own, as far as a merely human eye could see. There in Tarawa lagoon, in the offing of the native government station, I myself saw her floating, aureoled in the dawn-light, one morning not three weeks after Mrs. Grant had spoken.

A score of elder villagers came forward to back the old woman's identification and point out David's habitual mark, a big K deep-cut in the sternpost. She was half full of water: the Japanese guncotton had shattered her foredeck but, by some miracle, her bows had been left intact. Her mast, though

61

shaky, still stood. She had survived, by our reckoning, well over twelve months (meaning thousands of miles) of drifting, the shuttlecock of wind and cross-wind, current and counter current, through heaven alone knew what innermost solitudes of the central Pacific, to emerge out of that huge emptiness not simply within sight of Tarawa but inside its lagoon.

The odds must have topped hundreds of millions to one against her chance of ever returning, unsteered by human hand, from a point 400 miles away, to even the approximate neighbourhood of that single speck that was her birthplace. It staggers the imagination to guess at what they must have added up to against her chance of pulling off the 'double', which is to say, first the miracle of her homing and then the crowning marvel of her safe entry into harbour. In the whole twenty-mile length of the roaring barrier reef that shut her out from Tarawa lagoon, there were only two channels through which a human steersman could have brought her, half waterlogged as she was, unscathed. She either chanced precisely—just like that—on one of these passages and swam serenely in on the bosom of the rising tide, or else came swooping home superbly through the giant, charging combers over ten thousand jagged coral points and ledges, any one of which a few minutes sooner or later than the exact top of high water, would have ripped her to splinters in the crashing surf.

Mrs. Grant behaved most irritatingly about the whole thing, I thought. The wonder of it left her totally unimpressed. When I tried to bring it home to her, she only said I wouldn't have been so ruddy surprised about it if I'd been a true sailorman like her hubby used to be.

I'm bound to admit, though, that the old lady backed her convictions generously. Three beautiful spars of pinewood arrived at government station one day, with a note from her to say that as the government was holding on to David's boat, it might as well have these for nothing. They really belonged to David, she went on to explain, being as they were the last of the Californian lumber Sent Along So Special (the capitals were hers) for building the craft fifteen years ago.

I snatched at her gift. The gear needed to refit the *Flotsam*— that's what we called her—as the ocean-going sloop of my dreams was going to cost the whole of £50, which there wasn't a hope of Headquarters letting me spend out of public funds; and I couldn't afford anything near that amount out of my own pocket. But what with getting the spars so providentially for nothing and paying for the sails myself, I found it fairly easy to scrounge the rest from government stores—the odds and ends, I mean, like manila and wire rope, and rigging screws, and copper nails, and tackle, and muntz metal sheathing, and paint, and red lead, and tar. And what wasn't in stock to scrounge, I managed to find funds for in the grand old-fashioned way that district officers know, by sweating a pound here, a pound there, out of votes in the district budget intended for expenditure on anything but a local navy.

It was a highly illicit proceeding, but it did enable the *Flotsam* to go into commission almost at once as a despatch vessel; and, looking back at the service she gave us over the next twelve years, at the hundreds of sick villagers she brought in to Tarawa hospital from the other islands and the hundreds of pounds she saved us on their transport by trading vessels, I'm perfectly sure Heaven will be a more merciful judge of my crime hereafter than Headquarters would ever have proved at that time, had anyone on top been bright enough to detect it.

We put her on a monthly run to Abaiang, the island just north of Tarawa. When I didn't go along in her myself, the man who took charge of her was that superb sailor and wonderful friend of the Gilbertese, Chief Native Medical Practitioner Sowani, and when this happened, he and I would agree in advance upon a day for her return.

I remember it was the day before we expected her back

from one of those trips with Sowani that word came in of a man lying with a smashed thigh at Buariki, Tarawa's most northerly village. It was a compound fracture by the account.

The news had been relayed from runner to runner down Tarawa's 35-mile length. The passage across-lagoon was too rough for any ordinary canoe, as the south-east trades had been blowing hard for over a week. But our station canoe wasn't an ordinary one; also, a hospital dresser was going to take twelve hours to reach Buariki on foot, wading and swimming a dozen tidal passages by the way, and it's better not to keep compound fractures waiting as long as that in the tropics.

So there we were, an hour after the call for help arrived— the dresser, the station canoe captain and myself—clinging to a capsized canoe in a wild seaway, twelve miles from our starting point and eight from our objective. The going had been tremendous while it lasted, but even the morsel of sail we carried had proved too much for her in the sudden fury of a buster we hadn't seen coming.

The first thing to do with an overturned outrigger canoe is to get it completely free of the ghastly tangle of sail, mast and cordage that a capsize always produces. That done, you mount upon the upside-down outrigger float (as many of you as possible) and tread it under water. The deeper you thrust it, naturally, the more the bottom-up hull will be levered over to lie upon its cheek; and if you can keep that turning movement going, the float, travelling down and under, will eventually come up of its own buoyancy on the other side of the hull, which will then be right side up. After that, it takes no more than a kind of seesaw jerk that the Gilbertese use to flick half the water out of the hull, so that it floats again with a few inches of freeboard. The rest is child's play. The only condition is, you have to have fairly calm water to bring it off.

We did give the method a try-out that day, and we got as

far as righting the hull. But nothing we could do in that steep, savage sea would empty her of water. Then the tide began to fall, and we found ourselves being sucked nearer and nearer to the bellowing maelstrom of the barrier reef. There wasn't a hope of being picked up. Nobody was out fishing on a day like that, eight miles from land. But, oddly enough, I don't remember anyone feeling very panicky about it. This was possibly because death looks fearful to most of us only when we see a hope of escaping it, and seldom when there seems no hope at all. Or it may have been because, despite all appearances, something assured us deep down inside that all was going to be well. Whichever it was, when we had been four hours in the water, and had perhaps another twenty minutes to drift before the reef got us, the *Flotsam* came booming along. We didn't have to hail her: she was steering straight for us when Sowani caught sight of our heads— so straight that he had to alter course so as not to run us down.

The canoe was a total loss, as we had nothing to anchor her with; but we salvaged the spars and sail, turned the *Flotsam* north again, picked up the man with the broken thigh at Buariki, and had him lodged before midnight in Betio central hospital, where an immediate operation by Sowani saved both his leg and his life.

Sowani had finished his work up at Abaiang twenty-four hours sooner than we had expected. That was all there was to it, broadly speaking. All the same, one or two other details do seem to be worth mentioning: especially the timing of his start from Abaiang.

He had planned to sail at 7 a.m. and the mainsail was actually being hoisted at five minutes to the hour when he suddenly remembered that I had asked him to bring me back a dozen island fowls for the pot. He lowered sail at once and returned to shore. But the fowls were shy that day, bless their wild hearts! They came in so slowly that he decided to sail at 11 a.m. with only eight. In this way it came to pass that he left Abaiang neither a lot too early nor a bit too late, but at exactly the right moment, to ensure that the *Flotsam* would arrive, 19 miles out on her southward run, at the pin-point in space which we occupied at eight minutes past 5 p.m. after a northward run of about twelve miles followed by a westward drift of, say, three.

Then again, there was the whim that took Sowani about ninety minutes after his start, to enter Tarawa lagoon by the northern passage. He never could explain why he chose to do that: he knew perfectly well that his best course in that kind of weather was to stand on outside the lagoon, under the lee of the barrier reef, until he reached the southern entrance. But this would have brought him in five miles to south of us. So something obliged him to come the other way: or at least, this was how Mrs. Grant put it, and by 'something' she naturally meant nothing but the *Flotsam* herself. The craft had acquired a superhuman personality for her by that time. But for myself, I had no theories. I preferred to hug a single shining thought to my heart: the *Flotsam* would never have been there to rescue either our canoe party or the man with the smashed thigh if I hadn't had the good sense, a month or so before, to scrounge all that gear from the government. Heaven was obviously all out on my side against those asses at Headquarters. But I never made an official song and dance about that.

Years passed. Mrs Grant sold her trade store and retired to Australia. I had gone on to be resident commissioner, and a district officer who had better be called X— was at Tarawa in charge of the Northern Gilberts when that restless character Kaali, as the villagers called him, came cutting across the *Flotsam*'s peaceful and industrious course.

Kaali (for Karl) was the orphaned son of a Gilbertese mother by a German trader in the southern islands. Though his father had left him nothing but a quick wit, he had inherited a considerable piece of coconut land from his mother. So, as the

average islander felt nothing but respect for a tincture of European blood and he himself was never fretted by the slightest
wish to live the white man's life, there seemed no reason why
he should have failed to settle down happily in the carefree
environment of his lagoonside village. But he was always up
to mischief of some kind. The trouble for him was that he was
so charming about it; he was forever getting away with much
more than was good for him.

He had picked up a sound knowledge of marine motors and
boat-building while working for the British Phosphate concern on Ocean Island. This made him a most welcome guest
when, having got into trouble with the Native Court of his
home island, he was sent to Tarawa central prison for a change
of air. He was put to work at once in the station boat harbour.
He told me afterwards that his plan began to take shape the
instant he set eyes on the *Flotsam*. Something inside him
claimed her then and there for his own.

His first step was to tinker at the engine of an old wreck
of a motor launch that lay forgotten in the boat-house, until
he had it turning over as smooth as silk. That done, he proceeded to persuade X—, the district officer, that the *Flotsam*
would be the better for a bit of auxiliary power and that he,
Kaali, was the man to instal the engine. X— resisted at first,
but gave way in the end. I think I should have done the
same in his place: though the change reduced the cutter's
carrying capacity as well as her sailing qualities, it did make
her safer all round for inter-island trips in those low latitudes,
where the winds could be so variable, the ocean currents so
treacherous.

Kaali found it fairly easy after that to get approval for a new
suit of sails and, while he was making them at his own pace, he
cannily followed up the idea of all-round safety. His very
reasonable suggestion, which X— immediately accepted, was
that a case of bully beef, a couple of crates of navy biscuits and
a dozen tins of petrol should always be kept in the hold as a
reserve against every possible emergency.

The stores safely aboard and the new sails nearly finished, it was time for him to organize his getaway. The main point about this was that it had to be in the dark. He must be not only out of the lagoon but also over the horizon before day dawned to proclaim the *Flotsam* missing. So he got X— to decide in advance that, when the sails were ready, both these and the engine should be tested out on a trial run to Abaiang and back. His reason for choosing Abaiang was that X—, methodical man, always started his trips to that island at sunrise precisely, so as to arrive in comfortable time for lunch, and for this purpose he invariably had the *Flotsam* moored out at the end of the jetty the evening before.

Little remained then but to make sure of not being locked up in the gaol on the night of nights. He managed that simply by developing engine trouble, the evening he and Maamau took the cutter out to her moorings. Maamau was the policeman who acted as his overseer at the boat harbour all along, and had also been, incidentally, his willing slave and fellow conspirator from the beginning. While Kaali kept the engine making realistic noises at the jetty-head, Maamau came ashore and extracted authority from X— for both of them to go on looking for the defect all night long if necessary.

X—, whose house was down by the lagoonside, got so used to the sound of the engine that his ears gave up listening at last. It was the same with the sergeant-major of police and the chief warder of the prison. Not a soul noticed—probably everyone was asleep—when the noise stopped altogether. The moon set. In the dark of the night, the *Flotsam* vanished from Tarawa lagoon as secretly as she had entered it twelve years before.

When dawn revealed the flight, it was found that two girls of under twenty from Betio village had gone with them, persuaded, poor children, by heaven knows what glittering hopes of felicity and fortune down under the western horizon. Even Kaali, that bold planner, was never able to say exactly what he expected to discover in the blue beyond the blue.

68

Only, his pitiful ignorance was haunted by a dream that, in some western fold of space between the white man's country and his own, there was a land where things were different, where nobody would ever find him, where the mere ownership of the *Flotsam* would assure him and his party a position of authority and wealth forever.

They were unlucky from the start. The S.E. breeze failed them as soon as the first day dawned, and the engine began to play tricks on them. When it stopped, they were swept back by a heavy eastward set to within sight of the tree-tops of Betio; when it started, it carried them barely beyond view of the tree-tops, only to stop again. For the better part of a week they toiled to lose the land, but could not. It was as if the *Flotsam* was fighting against their struggle to get her away from her home. The battle lasted until their twelve precious tins of petrol were all consumed. By then the two girls, terrified, were begging to be put ashore again and the boys were doing all they knew to get them there. But it was too late. Wild weather blew up from the east and north-east; they were driven for five days and nights before it, four hundred miles and more deep into the solitudes where no land was. There the wind left them. They lay swooning for uncounted days in the fearful stillness of a sea of oil ablaze under the equator's savage sun.

They finished their last drop of water. Very quickly, one of the girls died. A torrent of rain came not an hour later to save her friends, but only for further days and weeks of torture. They thought no more of navigation; the mainsail was draped over the boom for shade; the fore staysail was rigged as a water catchment; only the jib remained standing. Drifting so, doomed puppets of the winds and currents and blistering calms of the doldrums, they came to the last few pounds of their navy biscuits. They were nearly dead on their ration of a crumb or two a day when the *Flotsam* found her end after eleven weeks at sea, smashed to splinters nearly a thousand miles from home on the reef of an island in the Banks group. The three survivors were rescued living from the surf, but the girl and Maamau died a few hours later. Only Kaali, the cause of all those deaths, came through. I never was keen on retributory justice for the simple-minded, but I can't say I much regretted seeing him shut up for three years on his return.

4

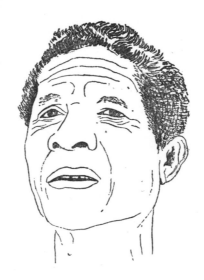

Arrests on Arorae

When my formidable first chief, E. C. Eliot, was teaching me
my job as a district officer in the Gilberts, he was fond of
saying, "You can't intimidate these people in the mass, so
don't ever be fool enough to try. It's their consciences you
have to work on when they get sticky; nothing else."

I didn't make much of his words at the time, but I had
occasion to remember them a few years later, while Eliot was
still in the saddle. It was when a sick and unhappy individual,
whom I shall call Albert, came trailing up to Tarawa from the
Southern Gilberts with a tale that the people of Arorae Island
had tried to murder him.

Albert was a stop-gap in the administrative machine. He
had been taken on locally as a temporary, provisional, acting

district officer at a time of desperate staff shortage. I never could fathom how my chief came to pick him. True, he spoke a bit of Gilbertese, but bully was written all over him, and his ranting talk about missionaries was a byword everywhere. To go and put him in charge of a tough, dourly Protestant crowd like the Southern Gilbertese was about as clever as setting a chimpanzee to play with a keg of dynamite.

Yes, Albert was a mistake—a private letter to me from the native magistrate of Arorae explained how enormous: 'He came among us breathing hate of our religion and shouting threats against our pastors,' it ran, 'and that was the beginning of our sorrows.' In other words, he had conceived a bitter jealousy of the influence of the London Mission's brown pastors in the southern islands, and was fool enough to think that bullyragging could smash in on Arorae. 'But,' the report continued, 'Timoni, the chief pastor, told us to be patient; so we suffered his talk in silence for a week and three days. And then arose the matter of Nei Tabita.'

Nei Tabita was a pretty village girl on whom Albert's roving eye had fallen. She, instead of submitting with joy to his forceful advances one evening near his house, stayed only to hurl a fallen coconut at him, then fled arrow-swift through the palm groove to the dwelling of her uncle, a native pastor. The pastor, a big man, came out and shooed him off with a broom and epithets of biblical frankness . . .

'So the day after,' continued the magistrate, 'he came to me, saying, "Punish me that insolent pastor." I replied, "For what crime in the Book of Laws shall I punish him?" He answered nothing, but the next morning he returned, saying, "You show favour to Christians. You are not fit to be a magistrate." And he pushed me out of my middle seat at the table of justice, forcing me to sit beside him. And, sitting in judgement instead of me, with a revolver before him, he sent men and women to prison for offences not named in the Book of Laws. And when my council of village headmen said "This revolver is not the Law," he sent them also to prison for

F

contempt of court. But because Timoni, the chief pastor, said "Patience! Keep the peace," we suffered that man for yet another four weeks and four days, lifting no hand against him. Nevertheless, our young men began to murmur, "If this is the Law, let us quickly make an end of it."'

The end came when Albert entered his seventh week on Arorae. I will reconstruct that final scene now from the notes I took later, on the spot. He had called a general meeting in the speak-house for more talk about the pastors, and a big crowd of men and women had turned up. But when he tried to address them, a mysterious sound arose: just a hum—mmmmmm—mmmmmm—from behind closed lips, untraceable to any particular part of the audience. He stopped talking; the hum stopped, too. He glared into their faces. Seated on the floor, they stared back at him, stony-silent. He began again: so did the hum. At a third attempt, he tried to shout it down; its volume grew to the bourdon of a church organ. It was the sight of him roaring and livid in his seat that at last broke up the peaceful game. A couple of youths burst into rapturous laughter. He whipped round to his wretched orderly: "Arrest those two!" he yelled. The orderly tried to obey, but men leapt up and held him off. And then Albert did the stupidest thing of his life: he snatched his gun from the table and pointed it at them. A woman screamed, "Death! He brings us death!" That loosed pandemonium; they all went berserk together: the whole audience charged. In a couple of seconds, he was down, stunned, under their trampling feet.

They would certainly have finished him then but for one lucky circumstance. Timoni, the chief pastor, had a wife whose colossal weight—$24\frac{1}{2}$ stone—was superbly matched by her agility and loving-kindness. She, seeing Albert's desperate plight, converted herself forthwith into a flying mountain of salvation. Her hurtling mass swept the astonished crowd back like flies from carrion. She fell upon the prostrate body. Albert disappeared from view. Timoni and half a dozen other pastors, ringing the two around, beat back all who dared to charge again with stunning two-handed swings of their enormous black Bibles. So it came about that Albert's life was saved by the very men whose influence he had come to break on Arorae. He woke up in Timoni's house. They kept him there, nursed, fed and protected by a continuous bodyguard of pastors, until a trading steamer removed him a week or so later.

The magistrate gave nothing but the barest bones of the last act in his letter. Also, he named no names. Clearly, he wasn't going to be interested in identifications later on. 'The table of justice was overturned upon me and I saw nothing,' he put it, and added, 'furthermore, I think that the only sinner in this matter was that man. This, I know, is not according to the Law. Therefore, I am no longer fit to remain in office. Therefore, I have locked away my uniform in the government safe and returned to my village. Farewell.'

The problem that his resignation had left on ice, for whomever it might concern, was packed into a neat postscript: 'The people say that that man was struck down by all of them together. They have sworn to resist anyone who comes seeking to bring this person or that among them to trial.'

The southern islands weren't my official business at the time; but there was nobody else in the Gilberts to do anything about it, and obviously something had to be done soon. Not that Albert mattered; he had pulled a gun and got his deserts. But it wasn't for the man in the street to decide who was guilty or not of near-murder. Only a court of law could do that. Someone just had to be brought to trial, unless mob law was to stand condoned on Arorae. This was the bone I felt I had better go and pick with them down there. And the sooner the better, I thought: Arorae had to be legally out of the red before Albert got through to Headquarters at Ocean Island with his side of the account. So I collared the only ship available—a small trading ketch—to take me south with my cook-boy, leaving Albert stuck in Tarawa hospital. The doctor

promised to hold him for at least a month. He was a pretty sick man, anyhow.

Our arrival at Arorae wasn't a triumphal affair; no canoes came out to see us ashore; we were dumped on the beach by the ship's dinghy. Not a soul but the ex-magistrate stood at the beach-head to greet us. He wasn't there officially, he said, but only to warn me against staying overnight.

"The ship's leaving me here for a month," I told him— "but where are the village headmen? Why didn't they, at least, come along? Or did they resign in a bunch when you did?"

"They did not resign. That man sent them to prison, as I reported to you," he replied, "and they are still in prison."

The futility of that angered me: I couldn't resist a savage dig: "I see. You left them sitting. You're out to protect the men who knocked him on the head, but you daren't release the men he imprisoned falsely. So you ran away. O, brave magistrate!"

He was a hot-tempered man. His fists came up and thumped his barrelled chest. The Gilbertese do that when they are on the warpath; for a moment, I thought he was going to wipe the floor with me; but he only stood glaring. I walked past him towards the island speak-house, usually so packed for visitors, now so forlornly empty: "Go and get your uniform on," I threw back at him, "then go to the prison and bring the village headmen here, also in uniform. Maybe we can straighten a few things out between us." It was a bit of a gamble, I suppose. But I was counting on his twenty-odd years of perfect service; and they did prove too much for him. Half an hour later, a fully constituted and uniformed island court was reinstalled in the speak-house. That was at least a beginning.

The district officer's first job on landing anywhere was to review the prison records. The court scribe brought the books along and the gaoler led in all the prisoners who wanted to appeal against their sentences. Arorae's prison population was five or six souls, on the average, but sixty-three men and women were lined up that day.

"Well, for heaven's sake, what is Natan in for?" I asked the scribe, starting with an aged fisherman, a very old friend of mine.

"For no crime that I know of," the scribe answered glumly.

"But what's in the records? What charge . . . what evidence . . . what did you write in the books?"

"Nothing," he said, and that ran for all the sixty-three. The records were just blank about them. Albert had dispensed with nonsense like charges and evidence. There wasn't a shred of a warrant anywhere for holding one of them in gaol.

I turned from the books to Natan: "Well, you tell me yourself how you got into prison."

"The white man came to my village, saying, 'You will be my fisherman,' but I said to him, 'I am a free man and I do not want to fish for you.' So he said, 'You are no longer free. I am taking you to prison.' And I followed him to the calaboose, for I thought it was the law."

I shut down at that point and delivered the lot from gaol. A couple of hundred sightseers had trickled into the speak-house

77

by then. Their collective regret for the attack on Albert wasn't going to be strengthened by a wholesale rake-through of his tyrannies—not, at least, if my own feelings could be taken as a guide. I sat loathing the thought of bringing anyone to trial.

More and more people came crowding in as I got on with the other court routines. There were seven or eight hundred of them at last, sitting with bowed shoulders crosslegged on the floormats. The quality of their silence, massive and tense, shouted its own warning. They were waiting for me to start trouble about Albert. Not that they gave a hoot for what I might say; they were there, on the contrary, to make that quite clear. Albert had destroyed white prestige for the moment. Any least reproach, or whatever it might be, of mine was simply going to be their cue for a roaring 'Hands off!' ultimatum. That grandiose showdown, nothing else, was what they were waiting so tensed for.

The only plan I had in mind so far was to avoid any such thing. Once they had struck their noble attitude officially, so to speak, nothing but the crack of doom would ever snap them out of it. So I hurried nervously on to the *rongorongo*— the newsgiving—with which a visiting district officer invariably ended his first day in court. It had to be got over. I burst into a spate of small-talk about the outside world, and for fifteen minutes they took it without a move. Then stirrings and sniffings began. I chattered on, my material getting thinner and thinner. They started throwing blank looks at each other. I began to repeat myself. I saw grim jaws slacken and gape. This childish gabble simply didn't belong—what could it mean? Had they but guessed, it meant I didn't know how to stop. I couldn't just get up and hop it, though I longed to; so I went on talking. How the deuce *was* I going to manage a smooth exit? I was at my wits' end by the time a man's voice interrupted: "But, Kurimbo! That man? We have a word to say!"

"Ah yes . . . that man," I said blankly, "yes, yes, of course

. . . that man . . . well . . . he's in hospital." As I paused, desperately wondering what to add, a great sigh burst from the mass of them. Now for the showdown, it seemed to breathe! But I had found a way round. "Yes . . . he's in hospital . . . at Tarawa. And talking of Tarawa, did I tell you this one?" It wasn't very clever, I grant you. I felt like a twisting rabbit. But believe me or believe me not, it stunned them. They let me go on about Tarawa for another ten minutes.

By that time I had dripped myself dry of ideas, and the only breakaway I could think of was to rush non-stop into an adjournment: I think my voice jumped a full octave with the strain of it as I twittered, "Well that's all about Tarawa and all for today so good-bye we shall meet again and you shall be blest." I was on my feet with the last words.

That too shook them deeply. They actually gave me back the traditional 'You shall be blest' all together, quite heartily, before anyone came out of the haze. I was almost clear of the speak-house when someone tried again: "But, Kurimbo . . . that man!"

The voice was definitely plaintive this time, which somehow gave me strength to answer quickly, "Ah yes, I had forgotten. Thanks for the reminder. Good Christians all of you. He also shall be blest." This floated me out.

They stayed dead silent for half a minute after I left. Then a woman screeched with laughter; men followed suit; indignant voices yelled reproof. The speak-house was roaring with the mixed din of mirth and anger as I crossed the island to the thatched rest-house by the eastern beach. It sounded as if they weren't all in one camp anyhow.

If anyone had ever thought of harming me, which I doubt, nothing came of it that night. I slept undisturbed to the surge and thunder of surf on the weather reef. But a visit from chief pastor Timoni had me up at sunrise. He, of course, knew all the facts of the attack and gave them to me freely. He named no names, however, and I didn't want any from him. You can't make a stooge of a missionary. Besides, the only radical cure for this trouble was for Albert's attackers to give themselves up of their own accord, and so short-circuit the foolish pact to resist their arrest.

That solution seemed beyond hope to me, but not to Timoni. "They would refuse today," he said, "because their consciences are still asleep. But later . . . when you have done your part . . . things will be different."

My part, according to him, was to awaken the general public conscience for a start. I agreed, "That's a grand idea, but how do I get them going?"

"Do as you have begun," he smiled: "ask no questions: answer no questions: say never a word about that man: nevertheless, go much among the people, laughing with them all the time. Do nothing but this at first."

"But, Timoni, why should being friendly start them thinking? Just the reverse, I'd have thought."

His answer struck me as more than a bit sententious: "They have taken the guilt of those men upon themselves, and guilt walks ashamed in the face of friendship."

"Hm? All right. So then."

"Then the people will begin to wonder aloud, saying, 'This white man is our friend. He loves to laugh and play on Arorae. Yet he continually hides something from us. What is it that he hides?' And one will whisper to another, imagining all manner of things, until at last they will send a deputation to you, saying, 'Grimble, what are you hiding from us?' And you will say, 'Nothing,' and they will go away empty, and the people will wonder still more, until presently someone will start a whisper: 'What is about to happen to us?'"

"But, Timoni," I objected, "where's all that going to lead us? Threats of danger or punishment just don't frighten Gilbertese men."

"Not your threats or mine . . . no," he answered slowly, "but the threats they imagine darkly in their own bellies . . . these they fear."

I put in a last objection: "Well, even at that, they'll never, never split on those men."

He shook his head: "Surely not. But those men themselves will come to you on a day, saying, 'We give ourselves up.'" In short, he was counting on their chivalry to do the only right thing, once they saw everyone around them sunk in despondency and alarm.

I admit it all sounded hopelessly far-fetched to me. But he knew and loved his own people, and he had given me a definite line, which seemed to be very much in keeping with my resident commissioner's ideas. So I promised to give it a trial.

There were many ways through to the domestic heart of most islanders in these days. The easiest of all began with the children. You had only to go and sit on the beach, pull out a piece of string and begin making a few cats-cradles to find them crowding round to show you how many more figures they knew than you did. Mothers soon drifted up to stand watching, then a few passers-by joined in, and so on, until at last you had a big sample of the village gossiping and laughing around you. A few days of that anywhere were enough, as a rule, to get yourself known for a private friend, whatever you might have to do there as a public officer. You could count on the Gilbertese being never less hungry for your friendship than you were for theirs. Remembering Albert, however, I couldn't believe it would work that way on Arorae.

But I was wrong. Perhaps it was nothing but curiosity that brought them along at first: it was a fair guess that I might give them more openings on the beach than in the speakhouse. Nevertheless, when it was plain that I wouldn't, they still came crowding to the five o'clock children's sessions by the waterside. A kind of island competition started to dig up string figures for me. I often imagined my severe chief saying, "What the heck are you doing to clear up this mess?" and myself answering, "Sitting on the beach, sir, doing catscradles." Only I never would have dared.

The single snag was, they stayed just as cryptic with me about Albert as I had set myself up to be with them. After ten days of nothing but smiles and gossip, I began to feel foolish. After fifteen, I was sure they were simply stringing me along. And then, suddenly, there were no more smiles or gossip: I went to the beach one evening to find nobody there. It was the same next day: I sat a long while waiting by my favourite canoe-shed and not even a child came along to greet me. I walked through the village on my way home. It was the friendly sunset hour when all the world was gathering round the cooking fires before the evening meal, the very time for talk and laughter under the trees. But nobody was laughing and, though they gave me gravely courteous greetings as I passed, their eyes fled mine and nobody paused in the road to talk. I thought the game was played out and went no more to the beach.

Another two or three days passed before I noticed those nightly rustlings in the bush around my house. I couldn't be sure what caused them at first—it's hard to tell one sound certainly from another through a curtain of surf noises and the hiss of the trees in the trade winds. I tried to keep an open mind for several nights—until, in fact, my cook-boy began to complain of ghosts creeping round in the dark. He rushed in one night to say he had seen three shadows crossing the pathway. I didn't believe in his sort of ghosts, but I won't say his alarm didn't get under my skin. I felt awful. The people were obviously up to something and it was lonely lying there wondering exactly what.

I had promised Timoni to keep away from him until he had something to tell me, but I thought it was time for another talk with him now. I sent him a message by my cook at sunrise, and he came at once. He would have come in any case, he said, because things were moving fast. Ever since I had started making friends with them, the people had talked with mounting wonder—just as he had predicted—of my strange silence about Albert. Alarm had soon crept into their perplexity. Within a fortnight, they were saying I had something dreadful to tell them—so dreadful that, loving them, I could not screw myself up to the point of telling it. "And now," said Timoni, "for a whole week they have been saying, 'We know the truth!' Do you remember speaking of warships?"

I remembered. Someone on the beach had asked me what a really big warship was like, and I had spread myself, trying to describe the terrible hitting power of a modern battle cruiser.

"Yes," he said, "that is what they are thinking: a battle cruiser will come and take you away from here, and when it is far out at sea—so far that none can see it—it will turn and fire all day and all night at Arorae, until not a man, not a pig, not a chicken is left alive. This it will do because of the injury done to a white man."

There had been meeting after meeting about it. The hundreds who hadn't even been present at Albert's downfall were asking why they should be destroyed with those who had. Others had put it round that I would stay and die with them rather than desert them in their extremity.

Well, there had been bombardments of islands within living memory, but none since the British flag had gone up in 1892, and I got nothing but shame and heartache from this horrifying rumour. So I asked Timoni to tell everyone he could, at once, from me, that there wasn't going to be a battle cruiser. He looked doubtful and answered gravely, "I will tell them . . . but they will only begin to imagine something even worse, I think."

It depressed me so, I forgot to ask him about my night watchers.

The first deputation came along two nights later—a dozen men in the prime of life, wearing the long white waistcloths of their island. They had a card to play and came to the point with a pitiful show of confidence: "Kurimbo, we have been thinking. We are here to offer a gift. In spite of what that man did to us, we are sorry for our anger, so we offer him twenty tons of copra . . ." They proposed, in short, to settle with Albert out of court, and no questions asked.

It was an enormous sum by island reckoning. I wanted them out of their misery, and the idea tempted me until my mind asked why the whole island should pay for the work of a few, and whose business it was, anyhow, to assess the damages. Then, because I had wavered, I answered tartly: "And what if he dies of his injuries? How much copra then? Or if not copra, who will pay the price?"

I wasn't trying to bluff them. I intended nothing but to blow their case out. But they read my rhetorical questions as meaning that Albert was dying or dead. Since the pastors had saved his life, nobody had conceived of that possibility. I saw their faces suddenly stricken with the thought: the murder of a white man. Their confidence fell away from them. I could see them thinking all together—Is he dead?—and not daring to ask, and wondering what would happen if he were.

I should have tried to knock the idea out of their heads at once; half of me wanted to, but the cautious half refused; I said instead, "As you're imagining punishments, remember what I told Timoni: no battle cruiser is coming to Arorae."

I added other things—Britain didn't do things like that, and so forth—but they only stared at me in sick silence until I stopped. And then someone whispered, so low that his voice barely came through the blanketing roar of the surf: "Kurimbo . . . you are our friend . . . what are you hiding from us?"

That 'you are my friend' shamed me into almost shouting the truth: "Don't be silly! I didn't say he was going to die. He's not." But, by that time, I might just as well have returned a blank "Nothing" to their questions for all the difference it made to them. They got up without a word. I heard their thudding feet on the run down the pathway as they raced to report to another meeting.

Next night, it was the magistrate alone who came. "Kurimbo," he opened, after some preliminary dithering, "what news have you for us?"

"No news at all for you," I answered, "except what I told those men last night." It was hard on him, perhaps, but his cock-and-bull stuff about seeing nothing when Albert was attacked still rankled. Besides, I wanted no official inter- mediary between the people and me at that point.

I was reading Francis Thompson two evenings later (it should have been his *Hound of Heaven*, I suppose, but it wasn't) when a shaky old voice from the darkness outside announced the arrival of another deputation: "Kurimbo . . . you shall be blest . . . we visit you."

The right answer was, "You shall be blest. Enter. Enter." As I replied, I set the hurricane lamp on the floor at my feet. Five old men, every one a friend, drifted in forlornly and sat crumpled on the mat beyond it.

Tobacco was passed round, pipes were lit: I talked banali- ties; they answered with tremulous courtesy: I talked on to those bowed white heads; and that is all that happened. Their illimitable good manners just would not let them pry be- hind the veil I had myself created. After a heartbreaking hour, I could keep it up no longer; a desolated silence fell upon us.

They rose unsteadily: "Kurimbo . . . we go . . . you shall be blest."

It was hard to see them leave like that, empty of all but fore- bodings. I called after them, "No warship is coming. No warship. Never. Do you hear?"

"We hear," one of them replied, but they read it as just another evasion: none lifted his head to smile at me as they drooped out into the darkness.

I went to bed, as miserable as any of them, and was half asleep when I heard low voices in the other room. It struck me that my mysterious night watchers might now be coming into action, as indeed they were, though not in the way I expected. I pulled myself together and went out with the lamp. Ten people were waiting there, grouped in pairs, the five old men of the deputation each with a younger man cling- ing to his hand. That way grown men had of holding hands always moved me with its innocence: I knew at once they had come for no evil; but I couldn't imagine what they wanted of me at midnight, and said so.

One of the elders led his companion forward a step or two: "This is my adopted grandson. These are our sons or grand-sons," he whispered, and stopped.

I guessed the rest before the young man spoke: "We have stood on guard about this house lest tale-bearers visit you by night, Kurimbo. And now we have come with our fathers and grandfathers to give ourselves up. We killed that man."

"You didn't kill him, you idiots," I remember shouting: "you didn't kill him; he's not dead; he isn't going to die." I kept on babbling just that and nothing else.

It got through to them at last. The old men were weeping. "Our sons will not be hanged?" "No battle cruiser will come?" "You are hiding nothing from us?"—the quavering chorus of questions broke me up completely. I found myself exchanging hugs at last with all of them, to get a bit of comfort as well as give it.

So the next day, the young men came to stand their trial before the native court.

The whole island packed the speak-house. A long, groaning sigh went up as they pleaded Guilty to a charge of assault with intent to wound. I could do little for the defence but plead the mitigating circumstances. I took the line that, what with the gross threat of the gun and the sense of total insecurity built up by Albert's doings, a very light sentence would suffice to meet the unintended excess of force used in the fear and passion of the moment. But the magistrate turned to the accused:

"Tell us," he said to the big, quiet youth who had disarmed and stunned Albert, "were you afraid of the gun?"

"I was not afraid, only angry."

"And what was in your heart? Did you intend to wound him?"

I cut in to say no law could oblige him to answer that

86

question, but he only smiled at me and turned again to the magistrate: "I wished to wound him. I tried to kill him. I was angry when Timoni's wife interfered."

"But you're sorry for all that now," I pleaded dolefully, for the record.

"I am sorry now, but I was angry then, not afraid."

The others followed his lead. What can a defence do for that kind of pig-headed candour? The magistrate gave them a year each.

My ship arrived two days later, and I took them with me to Ocean Island, picking Albert up from Tarawa by the way. My revered chief said he'd never seen such a ghastly mess as I had made of everything. My jurisdiction didn't run in the Southern Gilberts District. Nothing I had done had a legal leg to stand on. And why, oh why, he asked, while I *was* bouncing around the islands exceeding my powers, hadn't I exceeded them to the extent of reducing the magistrate's sentences at once? When I said I couldn't be defence counsel in one breath and court of appeal in the next, he said I was too damned legalistic for words. But it didn't really matter: he packed the prisoners back to Arorae within three months.

Pleasures of Polygamy

In the days before British rule came to the Gilberts, the son of a freeborn island family would usually take himself a wife when he was about twenty and she fifteen. It was part of the normal marriage contract that some of the ceremonial bride's younger sisters—or, if she had none, perhaps a chosen cousin or two—would accompany her as confidantes and helpers into her new home. In principle, their duty of loving-kindness towards her extended, when they reached maturity, as far as helping her to give nightly comfort to her lord and bear him children as he willed.

In practice, however, the average husband's initiative in this direction was severely crippled by his wife's. Not that she could blankly refuse him if, after several years of marriage, he proposed to elevate one of her companions to the honourable and permanent status of secondary wife in his household; only it was she, not he, who did the choosing, and her nomination ordinarily went to the least attractive of her sisters.

Gilbertese humour of old made much of this situation. The phrase 'a wife's selection' came into popular use to denote any young woman sadly lacking in charm, and the comedy of a disappointed husband's reactions, when confronted by a wife he feared with the lady of her choice, was a pet theme for the rollicking mime burlesques of the islanders. It made far richer slapstick than our own popular mother-in-law theme of Victorian days.

But the wife's choice was not, as a matter of fact, inspired by anything so unpredictable as female cussedness. On the contrary, it was dictated to her by centuries of sensible usage. The ugly duckling of any group of unmarried girls was obviously the one least likely to make an independent match of her own. She, therefore, was the girl to be endowed as soon as possible with a permanent, official share of her eldest sister's domestic felicity. Her more attractive companions could afford to wait— and were preserved at mint value, so to speak, by this arrangement—for offers of ceremonial marriage from outside. It was not until these reached an advanced stage of spinsterhood (say, at twenty years old, when all hope of their achieving primary alliances was lost) that their elder sister allowed them to become the secondary wives of her own husband.

The husband's function, in short, was to hang about in the background of the marriage market, faithfully fattening his wife's entourage of surplus females and steeling himself, honest soul, to cater personally for their fulfilment as women whenever Fortune or his wife might decide that nobody else wanted them. This again was a situation eagerly seized upon by the old burlesques. The scene mimed was usually that of a husband running around loaded with two absurdly shaped chunks of wood, which represented his wife's sisters, in a last wild bid to get rid of them in marriage to his rich friends. The comedy turned upon the gradual beating down of the bride-price from a fine piece of land to a single coconut and, finally, its conversion into a rich reward for anyone kind and courageous enough to take over the burden.

The only unqualified relief that custom offered a husband in the long run was the right to refuse secondary wifehood to any wife's sister who had ceased to be a maiden. The chastity of his

bride's companions was his peculiar perquisite from the start.
Cheated of this asset, he had no hope of marrying them off to
rich friends in exchange for desirable freehold properties. It
seemed to him unreasonable that any young woman who had
rendered herself unmarketable by private adventure should
expect him, the chief loser, to reward her in the end with a
position of dignity on his own permanent establishment. In-

deed, usage gave him the theoretical right to kill her out of
hand if—to borrow the Gilbertese phrase—she 'squandered'
his vested interest in her virginity. But here again his wife had
the last word, if only she hurried to intercede at once for her
sister. Custom not only prescribed a form of abject prayer for
her use in such an extremity, but also forbade her husband for
shame and pity to deny it. The island romancers of old delighted in tales of beautiful girls, daughters of chiefs, who,
risking all for true love's sake, and saved from death by the
pleading of devoted sisters, won through by this dangerous

road to wifehood at last with swains of humbler birth, to live happily ever after.

Stubborn Maiden

But real life had its romances, too. A regal old lady of Tarawa, Nei Taaruru, surrounded by her great-great-grandchildren, once told me how she, as a girl of perhaps fifteen, had won happiness with the mate of her own undaunted choice. It was a drama eighty years old and more as she spoke, and death in faction warfare had robbed her of her man long since. But the triumph of it was still fresh for her. Her voice rang so full and proud in the telling, I could picture her still for the gallant, flaming thing she must have been those many years ago.

I had said something about the amazing power a wife had, in the last resort, to save her younger sisters from becoming the mere chattels of men.

"Yes," she answered with a smile, "it was a strong power. Here I sit alive to witness it, who would have died but for the prayer of a loving sister."

She paused to think a little and then said, "They are all dead now. None will be shamed if I speak. Listen . . . this was the way of it . . .

"I was the youngest daughter of my father. We were a large family of girls. So, when my eldest sister married, I was taken by her with two others into her husband's house.

"And when I came to puberty, my sister's husband arranged a marriage for me with a friend of his. That man was a *toke* (chief), very rich in land, and he was willing to pay a great price for me. But he was old; his first wife was dead, likewise his second; even his youngest child was older than I. I said to my sister, 'This man is too old to give me children.' She answered, 'Be quiet. He will pay a big price for you.' I said, 'I do not love him,' but she closed her ears to every word of mine. And so it went on until the season of my marriage drew near.

"Then, because I could no longer bear my grief, I went to my sister, crying, 'I will not marry that old man. Let your husband kill me rather.'

"She looked into my eyes and whispered, 'You are in love with someone else. Tell me the truth. Who is it?'

"I answered, weeping, 'I love Tangaro and I will marry only him.'

"She did not scold me, but took me in her arms, saying, 'Tangaro . . . alas! he is very poor. When did he dare to speak to you?'

"I told her the truth: he had never spoken to me; but I knew he loved me, for our eyes had spoken to each other. It happened in the *maneaba* [meeting house] of our village, when I was brought out of my seclusion to lead my coming-of-age dance."

She meant by her seclusion the twelve months of segregation in the twilight of a triple-screened house, which every high-born maiden used to undergo as soon as puberty came to her. Protected there from all sunrays and carefully massaged three times a day with cream of coconut flesh, her body was gradually blanched from olive brown to the clear velvet gold of a peach. This was done to bring her complexion as near as might be to that of her people's hero ancestors, the fair-skinned, blue-eyed race of Matang, Land of Heart's Desire behind the sunset. And, while her skin was being made as smooth and white as a garfish's (so ran the island simile) she was taught the intricate gestures of a sitting dance composed for her coming-out. It was a dance which she herself was to lead one night in the huge meeting house of her village, seated in the torch-glare under the scrutiny, poor mite, of a thousand critical eyes, out in front of a triple crescent of seasoned dancers who took their time from her.

I thought, as old Taaruru spoke, that the young Tangaro's eyes must have shown very importunately to find and hold hers in the tension of that high ordeal. "*Bon te rine, ngaia!* [The pick of mankind, he!]," I prompted her.

She leaned forward to lay a hand on mine: "Somebody told you that? Yes, the very crest of the tree of beauty. No man was ever so beautiful or kind as Tangaro. My eyes saw only him that night. Every gesture of my dance was made for him." She laughed: "My sister's husband praised me at the end for the excellence of my *kateikai* [gestures]. That made me happy, for my heart said, 'What this man tells me here, Tangaro is thinking too, alone there in his canoe-shed.'

"But alas! though my sister's heart was sore for me, she feared her husband's anger and would do nothing to help. Time passed. The day set for my marriage was the first full moon of the season of Rimwimaata [The Scorpion]. It was very close when I made my last prayer, and my sister's patience ended, and she slapped me, crying, 'You little fool! You know nothing of love. You don't even know if Tangaro really loves you. Now be silent for ever!'

"I ran out among the trees. I did not weep. I said to myself, 'Nobody will help me. But if I were no longer a maiden, and that old man knew it, he would refuse to pay the bride-price for me.' I sat among the trees, thinking, 'Even if my sister's husband killed me for that, it would be better to die so than marry anyone but Tangaro.' I said to myself at last, 'So be it. Come what may, I will go quickly and ask Tangaro to spoil me for that old man. Then I shall die happy, all his.'

"I knew that he slept alone in his canoe-shed; most of the young men did so in those days. So, that same night, when everyone was asleep, I crept from the women's house and came through the bush to where he lay. I said only, 'Tangaro!' It was very dark, but he knew me. He whispered, 'I was sure you would come to me one night.' He took me in his arms and for a long time there was no talk between us. How wonderful, that! After so much longing to speak, no speech at all was all heart's fullness for us then.

"Then, with my head lying over his heart, I told him the whole of my thoughts. As I spoke, I heard his heartbeats race;

I knew his thought was one with mine; I said to myself, 'Let them kill me after this. I shall have belonged to him.'

"But when I had said my say, he was silent. He lay so long saying not a word that I cried, 'Tangaro, what is it?' Then, suddenly he sat up and pushed me away. His voice was angry when he spoke: 'Woman, you are mad! They will kill you if I do this thing to you.'

"So then I lied to him: 'Foolish Tangaro! no one will kill me. My sister has promised to intercede for me. It is quite certain I shall not be killed. Now take me for your own, and after a while, when nobody is angry any more, you shall buy me with a small piece of land. This is the way to win happiness in the end.'

"He only laughed at that. 'You are the foolish one, not I. Why, I have nothing but two pieces of land—one big, one small—no price for a chief's daughter.' And when I told him that nothing would buy me once he had made me worthless, his anger came back: he shouted, 'You are mad, you are wicked.' So at last I was angry and shouted too: 'You do not love me. You wish only to see me married to that old man. You refuse me because you already desire another woman.' At that he began to tremble; I heard his voice shaking as he spoke: 'Woman, I will not do this thing. It would be your death. But go quickly now lest I kill you myself for words you did not mean. Hurry.'

"I ran away weeping. But see! when I came near the village dawn was breaking. The women were already at work among the trees. They all saw me as I ran. They called my name. I knew then that I was as good as dead already. Who would believe that I had crept out like a rat in the night to return a maid? But I was not afraid; I was glad; I wished for nothing but death. I only wanted to make sure of being killed before anyone discovered that I was still worth the old chief's bride-price.

"So I said to myself, 'I will run straight to the old man's house-place. I will shout my shame there first of all, so that his people will try to catch and beat me. But I will escape from them and lead them to the house of my sister's husband. And we will all arrive at his door together. He will be so angry, he will kill me at once; and Tangaro will know that I chose death for love of him, and remember me with grief for ever.'

"Things fell out just as I had planned. I came to the old man's house-place. Men and women were standing round the house. I called to them from thirty paces off; I shouted, I screamed my shame. They ran towards me, crying angrily, 'Who did this thing to you?' I answered, 'A rat, but a better rat than your old chief,' and fled before anyone could take me.

"I led them to the house of my sister's husband. He stood outside. My sister and a crowd of people were gathered near him. They had been searching for me from before sunrise. Some people ran forward to hold me, crying, 'Alas! where have you been?' I shouted, 'I have been among the trees with my lover. He has loved me all night.' My sister's husband heard it. I called to him, 'Kill me now, for you will never get your bride-price.' Then the old man's people came running. They bawled, they screamed, they told of the shame I had done their chief. My sister's husband stood before me. He took my neck in his hands. 'Who is your lover?' I answered, 'A rat,' and spat in his face. He stopped my breath with his thumbs. A blackness rose up before my eyes. Then he let the breath come back. He said again, 'Who is your lover?' 'A rat, a rat'—I whispered, for my voice was sick. 'You die then,' he said and stopped my breath until the darkness closed over me.

"But behold now my sister, the brave, the tender-hearted! She sees me hanging from her husband's hands. I am nearly dead. She runs. She lies before him in the dust to make her prayer. Her head is between his feet. The head of a chief's daughter! His feet will trample it. How terrible that shame before the watching crowd—so terrible they hide their eyes; their hearts turn over for wonder and pity; they weep; they cry to her husband, 'Grant her prayer, we beg you, lest she

die for shame in the dust beneath your feet. Grant her the life
of her sister.' And he, for pride of her love and shame of
her shame, cannot deny her. His rage dies. He lets me fall
to the ground. He lifts my sister, saying, 'It is enough. This
woman lives. But take her out of my sight, for she is worthless.' And they carry me away to my house above the eastern
beach.

"My sister was sitting beside me when I woke. 'Alas,
Taaruru! Why did you lie?'—these were her first words, and
I knew she knew I had belonged to no lover. I was afraid. I
tried to speak, but my voice was dead in my throat; I could
only beg her with my lips, 'Don't tell, don't tell!' She took
my hand in hers, saying, 'Sleep now. I will not tell.' She
gave me water. My heart was at peace. I slept until the next
day's sunset. And when I could speak, I told her how Tangaro
had driven me away that night, and she wept with me saying,
'That is a noble heart! If only I too could have found such a
husband.' And after that . . ."

The old woman paused for so long, smiling at her memories,
I had to touch her arm: "And after that, Taaruru?"

She took my hand in hers: "After that there were goings
and comings and whisperings in secret for a year and a month;
but set all that aside; Tangaro bought me in the long run. He
could have had me for nothing, for all the value my sister's
husband put on me; but he said I was worth his big piece of
land, and I said the land I had from my father was enough for
both of us. My sister's husband was so pleased at that, he made
a friend of Tangaro for life. And so, at last, we were all at
peace together."

She fell silent again. I thought her tale was done and began
to thank her, but she reproved me. "Patience! This is my
sister's story as well as mine. There is better still to tell.
Tangaro and I were able to repay her in the end for all her kindness. Her husband died before she had borne him a child. We
took her into our house then, so that she and I could be
Tangaro's wives together. What happiness for all of us in that

sharing! He gave her children of her own, for love of both of us, so that her sons were mine and mine were hers, and we were one in him forever, and he was undivided in us until he died."

Unwanted Monogamy

Monogamy was forced on the Gilbertese by British law at the turn of the century, when Protestant missions had been at work in the islands for about fifty years, and the local administration for a decade more or less. There was no popular demand for it. On the contrary, except in one or two southern islands, tremendous pagan majorities still clung to the polygamy of their ancestors and the strictly controlled system of sex conduct that went with it. But nobody spoke for the pagans; the petition of the sectarian minority went through to London backed by the administration (so much must be said in fairness to the Colonial Office of the day), and that was abysmally that.

As soon as the new law came into local force, a multitude of women who had enjoyed the honourable status of secondary wives under the old system found themselves suddenly converted into potential adulteresses. That is to say, the criminal code of the day allowed of no distinction between the situation of a sub-wife and that of any ordinary breaker-up of homes: she could be brought to trial before her island court and imprisoned for common adultery if anything so contumacious as pagan love or loyalty tempted her still to cling to the father of her children. By the same token, the rising Christian generation was taught from village pulpits to call her children bastards, and did so, freely.

The pagans liked and admired the white man: not even this treachery could shake their incredible loyalty to him; so there was no attempt anywhere to rebel against the law. Only, after lifelong partnerships, hundreds of secondary wives were put away in shame by their men, while as many women, whose mates would have held them despite everything, returned to their villages rather than stay and be placarded as harlots. There were many suicides among the middle-aged.

A quarter of a century after the event, I talked with a pagan friend of Tabiteuea whose mother had preferred death by her own hand to living on, either in unlawful concubinage with his father or in desolation without him. Though she was only a sub-wife, she happened to love both her man and his ceremonial bride, her elder sister.

So she said one evening to her son, who must have been about twenty at the time, "Your father will be happy with my sister, and she will always be good to you for my sake. As for me, I shall be better out of the way, since the law has made a shameful woman of me. I go now. Tell them I died loving them."

The boy took her words for nothing but a cry of grief more bitter than usual. He put his arms round her, saying, "*Neiko* [Woman], we shall have each other. I will go and live with you in your father's village."

She smiled at him: "You are a good son," she said, returning his embrace. "Stay here and be a joy to your father." Then she walked out into the bush and hanged herself.

The next day, his father and aunt hanged themselves to the same tree. They doubtless felt, with his mother, that life was no longer worth living in a world of memories that the law had dishonoured for ever.

Looking back at the tragedies of depopulation caused by interference with the native custom in other groups of the Pacific, one is amazed at the vitality that enable the Gilbertese as a race to survive the murderous shock of compulsory monogamy. It is, indeed, true that the population figures showed a steady annual retrogression through the first dozen years of the new century; but the tide had already turned by 1915 and there has been a sustained forward movement ever since. I believe that this dramatic recovery was due to the unquenchable humour of the average pagan villager, which, as time went on, inspired him to escape from heavy new realities not by running away from them, but by using them, in the spirit of the old mime burlesques, as stuff for his Rabelaisian laughter. I have seldom seen a funnier piece of burlesque than one dating from the earliest 1900's (revised for my delight at Tarawa in 1925) in which a resident commissioner and a missionary, renowned both for their grimness and their intransigent dislike of each other, were mimed in the joint act of purloining forty odd sub-wives from the High Chief of Abemama and having them locked up for adultery—because they wanted the ladies for themselves. It was, of course, as untrue as it was indecent, but it left me feeling that nothing less than an angle of light could have inspired the gallant resilience of spirit which, under the very hammer-stroke of national disaster, had risen to make fun of the strikers.

Then again, the villagers soon realized that the law was an ass in action. Though it had formally banned a number of sex courtesies between 'in-laws' which pagan custom had honoured, its powers of prevention in practice were strictly limited. What its minatory clauses could and, very quickly, did do was to destroy the stern code of reciprocal duties—the moralities, in short—which conditioned the ancient sex-exchanges. These duties were too many and varied for their faithful observance to pass unnoticed, so they were jettisoned. But the sex-relations themselves were more easily kept secret, and the spice of danger added to them by the law's threats acted as a strong challenge to adventurous minds. Such affectionate mutual courtesies as the temporary exchange of wives between brothers or close friends were stubbornly maintained for many years after they became criminal offences. A new success-value was added to the villagers' lives—the psychological fulfilment of beating the ogre of the law in pursuit of love within the ancient pattern—and this compensated happily for the loss of the older values. It certainly drove them farther and farther away from the Christian ideal of sex restraint which (one must suppose) the law as well as the missions had in view; but it contributed as I believe, more vitally than any other single factor towards the rebirth of their interest in life among the ruins of their ancestral system, and so also, in the end, towards the survival of their race.

Tinaba

It would, however, be difficult to claim a universal moral rightness for all the old Gilbertese ideals of sex behaviour. Very few Europeans of my day felt any sympathy for the practice of *tinaba*, for example, or saw aught but good in the penalty of two years' hard labour that the law prescribed for it.

Tinaba was the reciprocal relationship between a young man's wife and his uncles, both maternal and paternal. The obligation which it imposed upon the young woman was one of unfailing *akoi* (loving-kindness) towards the uncles, extending even to the courteous loan of her person from time to time.

'From time to time' are meaningful words here. Two powerful restraining factors ensured that the ultimate surrender would be but sparingly demanded. First, there was public sentiment, which accepted the *tinaba* relationship only as a means of enabling a clever young wife to earn gifts of land for her husband from his senior kinsmen. An uncle-in-law who so lacked the quality of *akoi* that he attempted to make a personal romance of her dutiful solicitude towards him was in for a very bad time with his fellow islanders. Nothing stayed secret for long in the villages (except, of course, from strangers, white or brown). And, second, there was the ineluctable rule that the petition for her ultimate charity must never be addressed to the person one might have thought most concerned, namely, the woman herself, but to her husband. A wife suspected, in olden days, of entertaining private avuncular approaches, or even of knowing in advance that her husband was going to receive them, might suddenly find herself being strangled without the benefit of a trial. All this guaranteed her lord the chance of considering each application, as it came to hand, serenely uninhibited by the young woman's personal reactions. Custom gave him full liberty to refuse if he wanted to, and he would do so unless he saw excellent reasons for seeking or retaining the favour of the applicant. The lady had not a word to say either way; or if, in practice, she had several, the ages have left them unrecorded.

Tinaba was possibly an inheritance from remote ancestors whose ruling class commanded first concubitant rights over all the community's girl children, and therefore also the sole power to dispose of these in marriage. It was not uncommon, among primitive Oceanic societies, for political ascendancy to carry just such rights with it. If the ruling class I have guessed at consisted of neither kings, nor chiefs, nor even old men, but simply men of fighting age—which is another way of saying men of the generation of fathers and uncles among their fellows—the conditions basic to the practice of *tinaba* would be established. A young man's parents would naturally turn to their own brothers, his uncles, for backing when they wanted a wife for him; the uncles, on their side, would help them to secure the release of the desired girl from the women's house to the young men on condition that their own concubinary rights over her remained intact.

The next step would be the supersession of the original ruling class by conquerors of different culture; invaders, for example, like the latest known Gilbertese forefathers, the Breed of Matang from Samoa, whose chiefs never claimed common proprietary rights over the community's girl children. The advent of such rulers would put an end to the old system of *tinaba* as a matter of common law, so to speak, but by no means as a matter of domestic practice among the conquered population. In other words, the custom of uncle-right would persist privately, though its original, political *raison d'être* was no more. As time went by, its forms would begin to adapt themselves to the social conventions of the dominant race. The end product of such a process in the Gilbert Islands would be just what is found there—or, rather, was found in my day— that is, a system which had transferred all the real initiative from the uncles to the young husband, and which enjoyed the backing of public sentiment, mainly because it seemed a gracious and sensible way of getting elders, while still alive, to pass some of their wealth on to young married kinsmen.

It was impossible for a white officer to get to know his district intimately without becoming aware that none but a handful of truly devout Christians—perhaps five or six per mil of his parishioners at most—ever honoured the law against *tinaba* except in the breach. The same was true also of the gentler practice of wife-exchange. But custom gave a wife the right to withdraw from an exchange agreement whenever she liked, and, by blankly refusing to participate, on occasion she might even win merit in her husband's eyes. This put the ethics of it in a different category from those of *tinaba*. I was never in the least degree tempted to insist that the government's ban upon wife-exchange should be rigidly enforced, provided that nobody concerned in the arrangement was unhappy about it. This resulted not in making a dead letter of the law, but in confining the operation of its sanctions to cases in which undue pressure had been brought to bear upon an unwilling wife.

I didn't feel so easy about *tinaba* in my early years as a district officer. Though the law against it was a silly and dangerous mistake, nevertheless the implications of the custom—the idea of a husband having unconditional power to trade his wife for a price, even if only within a narrow family circle of bidders— seemed to me too repugnant to be altogether winked at. It wasn't until I tried to lecture old Moantau about it that I began to see things in a different perspective.

Moantau was a retired village policeman of seventy or more; a towering, bony old man as rugged of mind as of body, a staunch member of one of the Christian churches, and renowned throughout his island for the shattering honesty of his speech. It was chiefly on account of his bluntness that I chose him as a consultant: backed by his Christian convictions, he must surely give me some dynamic new ideas for the better control of *tinaba*, I thought.

I was, in fact, beginning to play with the notion of becoming an imperial meddler all on my own account; but Moantau, good old man, wasn't playing with me. Before I was half-way through my piece, he leaned forward from where he sat at my feet, seized my hand and began to chuckle. The chuckle grew louder as I tried to talk it down until, at last, it became a kind of asinine bray. I stopped and waited in furious silence for him to remember who I was. But he wasn't playing that game, either; he just went on braying and squeezing my hand until it suited him to dry his eyes on the sleeve of a white coat he was courteously wearing in my honour. "Sir," he quavered at last, "you make me laugh!" as if he imagined the fact might possibly have escaped my notice.

When he deigned to explain, I gathered that there were two things about me that amused him. One was my childish ignorance of what the women of his race felt for *tinaba*. Did I imagine, he asked, that the custom could possibly have gone on all these years, bang up against the law, without the constant collaboration of wives as well as husbands? Well, if I did, he, as an old policeman, was there to teach me better. And the other thing he found so killingly funny was the way I dared to say that all white people were shocked and disgusted by *tinaba*. Shocked? Ha! Ha! Disgusted? Ho! Ho! What words . . . what marvellous words . . . to hear from a race of men who themselves indulged in the indescribably filthy practice of brother-sister marriage! He proceeded to be contorted upon his guest mat with the joke of it.

I bit back my crushing denial until he was in a state to listen. But he recovered only to rob me of my thunder. He knew what I wanted to tell him, he said: the usual stuff about some kinds of brothers and sisters (he meant, of course, cousins) not being so much of one flesh as other kinds.

Not that he wanted to be unreasonable here, he added before I could get a word in. His own people had always permitted the marriage of cousins in the fourth generation of descent from a common ancestor, provided they were descended into *different* totem groups; but never, never, never between cousins, however distant, of the same paternal clan. Whereas we white men . . . we even married the daughters of our own fathers' womb-brothers! We pretended to think the flesh was different. But we must know in our hearts that words could make no real difference to flesh. Nothing but the lapse of generations could change the sameness of the skin, the hair, the blood, the bone, or the nature of the fearful sin of incest. So what sort of warrant had I, or any other member of a race so lost to sexual shame as mine, to come preaching to him,

Moantau, about being shocked and disgusted at a Gilbertese custom as modest as it was useful.

I am glad to remember having apologized heartily for my indiscretion before asking what his mission authorities thought of his views. Pressing my hand in silent forgiveness of the liberty, he replied without hesitation to the enquiry. "I do not share my thoughts about *tinaba* with the village pastors," he said sturdily, "for that is a family matter between me and my God. I am very sure that my God's heart and mine are at one in this thing." Which was, after all, not a bit more presumptuous than what we English (by which I don't necessarily mean Scots, Irish or Welsh) were continually thinking and saying in those days about the same God and *our* moralities, not to speak of our right to own an Empire.

So then there was nothing left to do but go and find a cure for my ignorance of what Gilbertese women (or most of them) really thought of *tinaba*. Old Taaruru of Tarawa was the one to help me there. She had told me her own love story a year or so before, and I knew from it that, even at past ninety, she still dwelt proudly on the happiness her long dead Tangaro had given her. My only worry, seeing how kind he had been, was that he had probably never dreamed of forcing her into any relationship that she disliked. And, in a way, I was right: he never had; only it had never occurred to either of them to dislike the *tinaba* relationship.

I chose the mid-morning hour to go to her *mwenga* in the village. She was always alone then, the children at school, the men and women out at their family tasks. That was a necessary discretion; but, seated alone on her guest mat, I knew her limpid and innocent candour well enough not to mince words. I can still see the astonishment of her vivid old face when I asked her outright if women who loved their husbands didn't hate the idea of *tinaba*. "Why, whatever should they hate about it?" she said, examining my features with care, as if for signs of mental disorder.

I tried to explain. But, under the scrutiny of those searching

H   105 old eyes, it was difficult to put the case as clearly as I had intended. I gave it up in the end, because she began to laugh, though not so loud as Moantau had done. "How wonderful are white folk!" she exclaimed indulgently at last, as if she were talking to a child, "So wise and kind in many things, so ignorant and cruel about family love!"

She fell silent, thinking, I believe, how best to make my dull mind grasp her people's point of view. Then she went on earnestly, "You talk to me of women. I cannot speak of others, but I can speak of myself. Perhaps if my heart is open to you, you will know the hearts of all my sisters too. Listen, then . . .

"I loved Tangaro, my husband, and I was very sure he loved me. But if he had never sent me to the sleeping mat of a *tinaba*, I should have died of shame; for, look you, it would have meant he judged me too ill-favoured to give pleasure to his elders, therefore loved me no more himself. Alas, also, I should have known myself useless to him—for what wife who gives no pleasure to her *tinaba* can earn gifts of land for the husband she loves and the children he had begotten upon her?"

"Yes . . . but, Taaruru," I remember arguing, "I'm talking of nowadays, not old times. No wife of today is allowed to earn those gifts of land, the wages of *tinaba*, for her husband. That's one side of the custom the law really had managed to suppress."

She smiled at me gently: "Sir, perhaps it is not as dead as you think. The *tinaba* gift can be called by any other name when the law is seen to be listening. Or it need not be a gift of land at all. Canoes, money, food . . . these are happy things too for a wife to earn for a husband, if there is love between him and her . . . and the law keeps no track of them."

I went on hurriedly to the next question: "But what if she bears a child to her *tinaba*?" I felt sure that in this at least she must see stigma.

But the European idea of domestic disaster just wasn't hers:

"The thing sometimes happens, indeed," she replied serenely, "and then the husband is happy above happiness, for the child belongs to him, being hers. The child also is lucky, because the mother receives for its heritage a special piece of land from her *tinaba*."

She told me then how, often, to avoid all danger of the law's suspicion, the child's real father would formally adopt it before the native court as his *tibu*, or grandchild—a thing anyone was entitled to do any day of the week. In this way, his gift of land to the mother would be made to look like an ordinary adoptive gift, and all the world would be happy, the brown men in their knowledge, the white in their ignorance.

I did manage to smile at that; but I hadn't quite got over the temptation to meddle. My mind was still looking for some ultimate insult to human dignity in the custom, and I thought the situation of an unloved wife really did show it up. I put the idea to Taaruru: a woman certain of her husband's love was one thing; but what of the woman who knew herself not loved? To be ordered out like that . . . no better than a slave . . . the fearful abasement . . . what bitterness of shame for her.

I thought I had made quite a case of it, for she did not reply at once. But there was something like scorn in her voice when she did speak: "Shame? A slave? Sir, you speak in white men's riddles." She checked herself and went on in a lower voice, once more as if I were a child. "There is shame when a wife goes out to deceive a husband—yes, even a husband who scorns her—for that is to become a rat. But how should she feel shame when she obeys a command from her *toka* [lord]; and when the flesh he sends her to meet is no stranger's, but his own; and when the words she speaks on that other sleeping mat are not secret love-talk, but the words of kindness that custom approves? These things make no slavery, no rat's work, for us. They make the duty of a wife who honours her husband. Do white men see shame for me and my sisters in that?"

Whether the likes of me saw shame in it or not struck me of a sudden as utterly of no account any longer. The only things that seemed to matter were her code of wifely obedience, austere and proud above the grasp of what I liked to call my civilized understanding, and, beyond that, the unshatterable integrity of mind that guarded her so safe from the petty physical shames of my imagination. "I see no shame for you, Taaruru, now that you have shown me a light," I told her.

She smiled into my eyes and then, in the swift absorption of the aged, forgot me for the work that lay across her knees. Her agile fingers, wrung by the rack of years, went racing through the countless strands of a new mat she was plaiting. I left her as her great-great-grandchildren came shouting home from morning school.

6

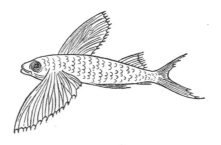

Defenders of the Faithless

It might well seem that the government's treatment of ordinary conjugal unfaithfulness, from the beginning, as a criminal offence instead of a civil wrong was just another piece of imperial arrogance as destructive as the banning of polygamy. But it didn't work out quite that way. The pagans approved of this particular dispensation as strongly as the Christian authorities did in the early days of British rule. Their argument started from the premise that death was the only proper sanction for 'rat's love'—except, of course, where the wronged husband allowed the seducer to comfort him with a large piece of real estate instead. The law having banned both private executions and expropriations of land for adultery, the least it could do now in the name of public decency, they said, was to prescribe heavy sentences of imprisonment for people who behaved like rodents.

I hesitate to claim that this excellent reasoning really counted for much in Downing Street. Nevertheless, the real motive behind the law was not entirely reasonless. The average villager, whether Christian or pagan, was apt to swing a very fast hatchet at a faithless wife and her seducer. Until his first anger cooled, the island lock-up was the only safe refuge for the erring couple. There is not a shadow of doubt that within, say, the first thirty years of British rule, the summary imprisonment of the over-adventurous saved many hundreds of enraged husbands from committing murder and, in consequence, just about twice their number of guilty parties from figuring as sudden corpses on the beaches of their islands.

But though this life-saving, murder-preventing policy, considered *in vacuo*, was its own complete justification, the trouble in real life was that our prisons were handicapped as corrective institutions by having to administer only the puny punishments allowed by British regulations. In the result, the law succeeded in robbing adultery of all its ancient terrors without providing anything like an effective new deterrent for those inclined to stumble. As a contribution towards the 'improvement' of national sex morals it was, in fact, like the law which enforced monogamy, a failure.

Sex and the Sabbath

The chaos of conflict between the new and the old moralities, enlivened by doctrinal squabbles between members of the warring Christian sects, was apt to throw up some original ideas as to the comparative gravity of sex offences in relation to other sins of importance in the Christian calendar. I shall never forget the one put forward by a cheerful young woman of the highly indoctrinated island of Beru. We met, when I was still young in my service, at a monthly session of her island court, she on her trial for a third act of unfaithfulness to her equally inconstant but still very jealous husband (who was there to give evidence against her) and I in attendance to watch her defence. She was likely to get as much as six months this time, unless mitigating circumstances could be clearly shown.

Things began to go badly for her as soon as she had been found guilty and it was time to consider the sentence. The

Native Magistrate asked her, idiotically enough, *why* she had committed her offence with the co-respondent, and she shocked everyone to the marrow by replying, as simply as a child teaching a smaller child, "*Nao* [Sir], because I love him," and laughing for the robust joy of it in his face. The husband shouted, "Alas! you see the sort of slut she is!" And then, for climax, it came out that every one of her three offences had been committed on a Sunday.

The court-house rustled with horror and delight. I had no real hope left of helping her after that. But I wanted to keep her talking, just in case. So I observed—with reference to the despotic sabbatarianism of the Southern Gilberts in general— that the Tempter always would find mischief for idle hands to do.

It wasn't a popular remark. I felt some of the court's disfavour being immediately deflected from her to myself; it was clear from her looks that even she felt I had said something pretty shocking. I decided to plug away at the idea nevertheless, and went on to recommend a bit of sewing or other useful work as an infallible defence against temptation, whatever the day.

She had managed to listen in silence so far, but this beat her: "Sir!" she burst out, forgetful of all but her moral indignation. "You must know as well as I do that it is a deadly sin *to work* on the Sabbath!"

Both the court and the audience practically roared their approval of the snub. On my own defence now, I pointed out rather sheepishly that, after all, the other thing was a sin too. But not a breach of the *third* commandment, they told me with heat—only a breach of the *seventh*. It was a far, far better thing she had done, in fine, than the thing I had suggested she ought to have done, and she got off with three months on the strength of it. The only party who finished really annoyed was her husband.

Forgiving Sinner

Poor pretty Marina of Tarawa found that not even the walls of our central prison made sanctuary enough, back in 1916, to save the tip of her impudent nose from amputation. The government's extreme poverty was the real root of her trouble: we simply could not afford big prison staffs in those days. It followed that our cheerful brown wrongdoers roamed the government station from sun-up to sundown doing outside chores almost wholly unguarded. Not that they disliked their all-but-freedom under the whispering palms; but it suited Marina's husband too well: he had only to stroll into the station and spy long enough from behind some bush to see exactly when she separated herself from her working-party.

She had been set to weed a path by my office the morning he chose to strike. But a sister of hers from the village had kindly dropped a pipe of tobacco and matches beside her as she worked, and what could a poor girl do then but fall to the temptation. She grabbed her contraband treasure and made for the seclusion of a clump of flowering *uri*-trees fifty yards from the office.

I don't know how long she had enjoyed her smoke in the scented shadows before he was upon her. It was her rending screams that first brought me and the office staff rushing into the picture. We found her lying in a welter of blood under the *uri*-trees, her cotton jumper off and held against her face. "Bairiu! Bairiu! (My nose! My nose!)" she was moaning as I knelt on the sand beside her.

Not to put too fine a point on it (if I may use that expression here) the tip of her nose was gone. Her husband had bitten it off. It was one of the things short of murder that jealous husbands sometimes did to fickle wives—an absurdity and a horror grossly compounded. But it did not spell tragedy for a heart as stout as Marina's. Even in the extremity of grief for her broken beauty, she lost neither her head nor her humour.

"He spat it out at me before he ran off, saying, 'Do what you like with that!'" she told us with a faint giggle, as she stood up and walked off to hospital. "Perhaps, if you can find it now, Doctor Sowani will sew it on again, and it will stick, and that man will be somewhat disappointed."

None of us had the smallest hope of any such miracle for her, but we did start a search and presently someone found the piteous fragment. Within half an hour the doctor—or, rather, Chief Native Medical Practitioner Sowani, the mainstay of Tarawa hospital and trusted friend of all the islands—had it back in its place again. Yes, and, by heaven! Nei Marina's gallant faith in him proved utterly justified. I don't know whether he sewed it on or merely used adhesive tape, but it did most gloriously stick.

The nose came out of hospital slightly changed in shape, but what it had lost in academic beauty, it turned out to have gained a hundred times over in glamour. It became the first wonder of Tarawa. Visitors from all the group came to look at it. A number of young men offered to marry it. But, as she pointed out, the repaired job still belonged to her husband. He hadn't started divorce proceedings and she certainly didn't intend to take any against him, she said.

I had a long private talk with her shortly before her husband was brought to trial for malicious wounding. She was by then passionately against the idea of a prosecution. I like to dwell on this part of the story. Her argument was that he would never have been tempted to bite her nose off but for her initial unfaithfulness. Therefore she herself, not he, was the one to blame for the whole thing. And now that he was good enough to want her back, unclean, self-spoiled thing that she was, why should the law come butting in to punish him?

Well . . . who was a district officer to interfere with a wife's conscience or call her generous constancy in question? I didn't try to do so, but pointed out instead, that she herself was, so far, the only known witness against her husband. He had been found innocently working on his own land after the assault.

This evidently stuck in her mind because, when he came to trial before the Native Court, she testified on oath that she hadn't really seen the man who had bitten her and hadn't recognized his voice either. As nobody could catch her out, and her previous allegations had been quite informal, and the accused had a copper-bottomed alibi anyhow, he left the court without a stain on his character. It was rank perjury all round—I haven't a doubt of it; but, legal quibbling apart, what is ultimate truth? Nobody knows for sure, but people have visions of it and Nei Marina clearly valued hers higher than a bite in the nose. Perhaps she confounded it in her poor simple heart with such things as love, and love again with such things as humility and forgiveness. But I can't swear to that. What I can vouch for is that it led her back to her man. She and he lived very happily together from that time on.

No Pagan Hanky-Panky

It is worth a man's while to remember now that erring wives did not entirely monopolize the Gilbertese market for generosity: not, at least, at Tarawa in 1916. There was Taratake, for example, a much wronged husband. Taratake knew of his own goodness that, only given time to cool down, he could condone practically any slip of Laughter-of-Waves, his wife. So he brought her to my office one day, saying, "Kurimbo, this woman has sinned. She has already deceived me twice before, and I have forgiven her. I love her greatly, as all men know, and I wish to pardon her again in the end; but I fear I shall strangle her this time unless you lock her away from my anger for at least six months."

I asked Laughter-of-Waves if the proposal struck her as reasonable. It did, she said. She didn't want to be strangled; besides which, both she and her partner in crime were sorry for what they had done and eager to afford Taratake the solace of an official expiation. I accordingly recommended the two offenders to the favourable consideration of the Native Court, which obliged all of us by sending them to prison for six months each.

Taratake's only real fault after that was too much forgiveness. Yet can there ever be too much? And then, who but a complete saint could have turned a blind eye to the interior weakness of our penal organization? The colony was desperately poor. Big prison staffs were entirely out of the question. We were happy indeed, in the circumstances, if our criminal gentlefolk were tactful enough to keep their breaches of discipline decently hidden and beyond that, willing, when they chose to sing at night, not to bawl themselves quite hoarse.

Taratake had once done a year in the central prison at Tarawa (I forget what for) and he knew much more than I did about its interior possibilities. This valuable experience, plus his wife's clever use of the latitude allowed for midnight song, plus the happy accident that the women's wardress was his father's sister, enabled him to organize the sort of reconciliation that his generous heart ached for.

I only began to learn the facts when Laughter-of-Waves had been released from prison for some months, and I heard that she had given birth to a fine son. That was pleasant news in itself, but a question of time rather puzzled me. The prison records said that she had been discharged just five months and three weeks previously after serving her full sentence of six months. It made strange biological arithmetic for the cloistered seclusion of a female prison, unless one believed in spontaneous generation. I asked them to come and have a private chat with me. The baby came with them.

Our opening talk was about a virgin known to Gilbertese mythology as Nei Matamona, who—so the story ran—had once upon a time been visited by a sunbeam as she lay basking in a solitary pool, and so became the mother of that mighty sun-hero Bue. But Taratake said No: as a Christian (though his wife was a pagan) he couldn't approve of Nei Matamona's methods and didn't, in any case, believe things happened that way nowadays. There was clearly nothing to do then but apologize to him at once, on behalf of the Secretary of State for the Colonies, for what had happened to Laughter-of-Waves in the female lock-up and congratulate him, in the name of humanity, for his generous readiness to father an interloper's child.

This was, however, more than a virtuous mother could take in silence. Laughter-of-Waves spent the next ten minutes forcing me with floods of indignant tears, to note the astounding resemblances between her baby and his father. All that time, Taratake sat with an arm round her waist, nodding his head at every point she made and shaking it with such reproachful eyes at me that I felt lower than a worm. But I did want all the facts, if only for the appraisal of my own gullability, and presently they came tumbling out.

It appeared, to begin with, that Laughter-of-Waves was a most accomplished sorceress. Her spells, she claimed, had twice won Taratake's instant pardon for her wilful ways; it was therefore only natural to turn to them again for help in prison. She didn't want him throwing eyes at other women while she was locked up; wasn't she right in that, she asked. I had to admit I thought she probably was, and was glad to hear from her then that the gaol wardress, Taratake's aunt, had held absolutely the same opinion.

It was this aunt who had obtained from him a few strands of his hair for the right kind of spellbinding and had also provided matches for burning them at the right ritual moment. Laughter-of-Waves herself had organized the community singing. "Do you remember," she reproached me, "you once sent your cook over to us three nights running, to beg us not to sing like lunatics? You see, everyone had to sing loud. Otherwise, they would have heard the words of my spell, and it wouldn't have worked." She was good enough, after hearing my expressions of regret, to let me have the words in question. Here is the slightly expurgated English rendering of them:

Mr. Hair-of-his-head, Mr. Hair-of-his-head,
Go you to him, to Taratake!
Whisper my name when he dreams, when he wakes,
When he walks among the women.
Draw him by the hand,
Draw him by the foot,
Draw him by the heart and entrails to me.

He thinks only of me;
He dies for love of me;
There is no woman for him but me, no love but mine, no
    love-making but mine.
He comes to me, he comes, he is here with me,
With me, Laughter-of-Waves-o-o-o!

The burning of a single hair at the end was enough to speed
the indwelling spirit on its way.

I don't know how it strikes you, but I thought it pretty
natural, that, after three performances of a ritual like that,
Taratake should have started dreaming of his wife—especially
as he knew from his helpful aunt exactly when the series began
and ended. The third performance completed, he said, he had
allowed Mr. Hair-of-his-head one night to come and draw
him by the hand, a second to do the same by his foot, and a
third to deal with his heart and entrails. "But, Taratake," I
ventured to protest at this point, "you're a Christian! You
can't go playing about with pagan spirits like that, you know."
The dignified reproof in his answer left me sorry I had spoken:
"Sir, you have forgotten that it was my own hair. The spirit
of it was as Christian as I am myself."

So, on the fourth night, the spirit led him to the wardress's
quarters in the gaol yard. It was easy going after that, because
another spell known to Laughter-of-Waves held his aunt
bound to her mat in a miraculous sleep. This again was,
religiously speaking, blameless. She was a Christian like himself and had given the sorceress some of her own eyelashes for

the sleep ritual, so as to make sure there was no hanky-panky with pagan spirits. Comforted beyond measure by this thought, he took the key she had carelessly left by a lighted hurricane lamp and pressed serenely on with his mission of forgiveness into the female lock-up.

Everything was ready for him there. The other lady inmates had plaited garlands of perfumed flowers to hang about the room. They lay now, magicked asleep, on the concrete floor. They had to be on the floor, because their wooden pallets were needed to make the little cubicle where his beloved awaited his forgiveness. But what could hard lying matter to them, who slept so fast and dreamed so deep, maybe, of love fulfilled in the scented darkness?

"And how many times did they have to be magicked altogether?" I asked Laughter-of-Waves when all was told.

"Only six," she replied. "You see, it was difficult. We started the night you left on a visit to Abaiang and finished the night before you came back. You wander round the station a lot at night, and we didn't want to hurt you."

I was grateful for their tender feelings. For the rest, what was to be done? One can't wheedle confessions from one's parishioners only to put the dogs of justice on their tracks. So I asked them weakly what their idea of a fair thing was. They had it all ready: "We thought," said Taratake, "that it would be nice if we called our son Kurimbo, after you." I looked at the brat. He really was rather a nice baby. I was proud to be his sponsor.

The Thank-Offering

As a rule it was only when a husband suspected his wife of unfaithfulness that he took a knife to her admirer. But Terara's jealousy went a step beyond that. Though he knew perfectly well that his exquisite, shy South-Wind loved him with all her heart (he admitted as much at the trial) he could not resist having a stab at Aimoa for merely making sheep's eyes at her. Aimoa nearly died of it and Terara was lucky to get off with only a year's hard labour.

The trial took place on Kuria Island, where the two young men and others—all of Tabiteuea—were working under indenture for old George Murdoch. But Terara couldn't be held in the local calaboose, because the only gaols authorized to take in long-term prisoners were those at district headquarters. I was bound to take him with me to Abemama (for that was in 1917, when I was district officer, Central and Southern Gilberts) and this brought up the question of poor little South-Wind. She begged not to be sent back alone to Tabiteuea. Not that she was afraid of her natural guardians, Terara's mother and sister, she said; she knew they would be very kind to her; but Terara, in prison all those hundreds of miles away at Abemama, would die every day anew of grief and jealousy, wondering, wondering what she was up to out of his sight; and she herself would die for thinking of his misery and pain. Couldn't I possibly manage to find some job for her at Abemama, so that she could at least show herself to him every day?

As it happened, my station sergeant Rota had just married a wife much younger than himself and was only too glad to find a nice companion for her, rationed by government, against the times when he had to go on tour with me. So we took South-Wind in with us, and she was a tremendous success all round at Abemama. Mrs. Rota loved her at first sight, and so did the wife of the warder of the men's gaol, which was even more important. She was allowed to sit in the warder's house every morning at six o'clock, to smile at Terara as he passed out of the prison yard with his working party. This and the usual visits allowed by law seemed to keep him very happy about her, for he sang and laughed all day at his work with the most carefree of his fellow boarders.

About a quarter-way through his term, he came to my office for a private talk. It appeared that he thought himself indebted to me for everything Rota and his wife were doing to keep South-Wind happy. It had been on his mind for a long time, he said, and he wanted her to start getting level with the account as quickly as possible. With 100 per cent good conduct marks, he would be out in six months or so. Wasn't there some regular job of sweeping or scrubbing or sewing that I could give her to do for no pay in the meantime, so that he could be sure she was at least earning her board and keep with us? People had their pride, after all.

So South-Wind, a glowing wisp of loveliness no bigger than an elf, became cook's mate, yard girl, scullery maid, washerwoman's help, waitress, sewing maid, and despatch runner in our establishment (Olivia was with me in those days) and very efficient she was in every department. Only, we couldn't swallow Terara's notion of her doing it all for nothing and, as she raised no personal objection whatever, we gave her the princely wage of five shillings a week plus, of course, the run of her shining teeth in our larder.

She, wise child, told Terara nothing about the pay packet until he walked, a free man, out of the prison and into the warder's house, where she was waiting for him. She had to tell him then, to explain how she came by the magnificent pile of gifts—a new pipe, fifty sticks of tobacco, a brush and comb, a safety razor, a bottle of hair oil, two pounds of fish line, a mouth organ, a tin of boiled sweets, a flaming orange waistcloth length, and I don't know what-not else—that she had set on the mat for his sweeter welcome back into her arms. All but a few shillings of her wages had gone on them, and £6 had a lot of buying power in those days.

We gave them a house in the police lines and found a paid job for Terara in the station carpenter's shop until we could ship them back to Tabiteuea. All this was pure routine; we did the same for every discharged prisoner awaiting repatriation; but Terara had his own views about it: I simply couldn't get the idea out of his head that he owed everything to me. He would come along to see me, bringing South-Wind with him, three or four evenings a week, and every time he would harp on the depth of his indebtedness. I liked his visits very much; he was one of those rare Christians of the younger generation who refused to see shame in the traditions of his pagan ancestors; but I did find his misplaced gratitude infinitely tedious, and at last I couldn't resist telling him so.

I was sorry at once that I had spoken. I could see from the silent look he gave me that he was badly hurt. All he did for reply was to take my hand, lay it palm down on his bent head and say, "You are my father; I am he who lives in your hand. So be it here, where I am a stranger; but it shall be different at Tabiteuea, lest I be shamed forever." They left at once and I did not see them again until we were all aboard the schooner *Motau*, southward bound for Tabiteuea, via the islands.

A couple of nights out, both of them and Rota and I were together on the foredeck. Sprawled on our mats, looking up at the mastheads dancing among the stars while we drank great draughts of the milk-white wine of the moonlight, we talked from the depths of silver peace that only the moondrunk know, of ghosts we had seen, and mysteries wondered at, and strange things heard report of out of the enchanted past. It didn't strike me as a bit out of place, therefore, when Terara started to tell Rota of a marvellous dream he had had just before leaving Tarawa. It was a dream of a shining white frigate-bird, surpassingly beautiful, that had flown down from the sun and settled on his breast. Happiness like a surge of the ocean had swept through his heart at that, he said, and he had cried aloud to the bird, "O chief from the sun, you have come down from your height to me, who am nothing. I threw away all I had and ran upon death; you saved me and gave me back my happiness. Now, before you leave me never to return, accept from my hand one token of love and thanks beyond words. So, I shall be forever free of a debtor's shame in remembering your loving-kindness."

I did realize before he finished that it hadn't been a real dream at all. He was simply back on the hobby-horse of his

I

perishing gratitude, and I in person was this paragon of a bird he had been burbling about. I should probably have said something pettish had not Rota, to my surprise, turned on the anger instead of me. He started to go bald-headed for Terara, calling him insolent, and shameless, and pagan, and half-a-dozen other names for daring to talk like that before the Man of Matang. He was so rude, I had to protest at last, "But, Rota, there was nothing insolent or shameless in what Terara said. You're being very silly. Dry up and I'll talk for myself if you don't mind."

Turning to Terara then, I tried to comfort him: "I shall be staying tomorrow night at Nukunau. Come ashore and see me in the evening, and we'll think together of something you can do for me. Bring South-Wind with you." Having said which, I got up and went to bed before either could speak another word.

Rota was sulky all day at the Nukunau rest house, especially when, after my evening meal, he came to take orders for the next morning. He practically ran out of the room without saluting as soon as my cook-boy came in to spread a guest mat at my feet as I sat in a squatter's chair and to tell me that Terara and South-Wind had arrived.

Poor South-Wind was a sad sight when they appeared, her lovely little golden body all dolled up and extinguished in the frilled horror of a mission-school Mother Hubbard. But it was high ceremonial dress in the southern islands; she had clearly put it on in my honour and I did manage to say something nice about it. I thought it was her pleasure at the compliment that made her more demonstrative than I had ever before seen her. Instead of sitting down on the guest mat to face me with Terara, she sank to the floor by my feet, facing the guest mat, her right cheek resting like a child's against my knee. I must say I liked it a lot. But, remembering her husband's over-jealous knife, I couldn't help hoping hard that he trusted me as much as she did. And then I noticed that he was still standing.

Before I could bid him be seated, he stepped forward and

laid a wreath of white *uri* blossoms on South-Wind's head. "I leave this woman in your hand tonight. Let her loving-kindness be to you the measure of my gratitude," he murmured, smiling serenely down on both of us. I was still gaping at that when he added, "For twenty days I have slept apart from her, so that she might come to you without shame."

I sat cursing myself for a fool. This was the token of love and thanks he had meant the night before. No wonder Rota had been scandalized. But how could I turn and rend him now after inviting him to bring South-Wind ashore to me? He couldn't possibly have guessed that I hadn't meant it this way. Besides, now I understood his offer, I couldn't agree with Rota: I still could see no insolence in it—nothing indeed but a gesture of regard that wrung me with its generosity. My mind groped desperately for some way of refusing that might not smash his pride.

But all my clumsy talk of the difference between his people's customs and ours seemed to leave him more and more crestfallen. I could not arrive at convincing him that my rejection of his most precious gift was due to no fault in himself or her. I don't know how I should ever have comforted him without enlisting South-Wind's help. She had sat silent throughout, her cheek still against my knee, her right arm crooked around my calves. I think the contact must have enabled the passage of an inspiration from her to me, for I was somehow certain of her answer when I said, "Tell us the truth, South-Wind, tell us nothing but the truth: did you in your own heart really want this thing?"

She turned her head and laughed up in my face: "Not I," she replied, then looked across at Terara accusingly and added, "That man knows I did not want it. I said to him, 'If you must send me to another man, why must it be a white man?' I also said, 'This white man is not like a frigate-bird but a . . .'"

Before she got the word out, Terara sprang forward with an indignant bellow and clapped his hand over her mouth. I never found out what she was going to say, but Terara knew, and her rejection of me to my face, so much more outspoken than mine of her, seemed to inspire him all at once with renewed self-respect. He raised her to her feet, laughed down at me with the air of a man rid of a burden, picked her up in his arms, pagan fashion, as if she were a bride new-wed to be carried across his threshold, and ran out with her into the flaming moonlight. A minute later I heard Rota hoot with laughter from the kitchen. There were no more puritanical sulks from him the next morning.

7

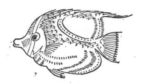

Pig-Time Money

I had been only eight months at work on the lands commission when, in 1923, shortages of staff forced Reggie McClure to order me back to district duties. Though I had waited years to get the commission started, this interruption wasn't on the whole unwelcome: a sorcerer's revengeful trick up north[1] had recently done queer things to my insides and these had need of all the doctoring they could get at Tarawa central hospital. I should have felt more troubled had it been revealed then that I was never again to sit in my beloved lands court. For one reason and another the commission was not to be re-opened until years after the Gilberts had seen the last of me. But that is a tale for someone else's telling.

Almost as soon as I was out of the doctor's hands at Tarawa, the big ship arrived. She was a beautiful new non-British super-tramp of 11,000 tons come to pick up copra from Burns, Philp & Company's big island depot at Betio, and her captain, who spoke fluent American-English with a strong accent of his own, was one of the most lavish entertainers I have ever met. Three days on end, refusing every invitation to partake of our jointless, greenless, fruitless hospitality ashore, he regaled the

[1] *A Pattern of Islands*

senior medical officer and me at lunch with lordly thick beef-
steaks, ineffable salads and lashings of good liquor in his sumptuous quarters on board. This was, I think, the first time since
creation's dawn that the air of Tarawa had swooned to the
deep, the holy, fragrance of *filet mignon* grilled *à point* or thrilled
to the crisp lilt of lettuces munched dewy-fresh from the cool-
room. It was certainly the first and last time I ever tasted such
bliss within two thousand miles of Tarawa.

We soon learned that this unparalleled abundance came to
us out of the shipowner's pocket, not the captain's. His chief
pleasure in heaping all these good things upon us was, in fact,
to demonstrate what a superior good fellow his employer
was.

"You Pritish haff no shipowners so chenerous as ours,"
he kept saying as he practically pushed second goes of everything down our throats—"You Pritish yoost don't know how
to run ships like vee do." And his huge frame rocked with the
roaring fun of it when we, all too painfully aware of the faults
of our local shipping concerns, told him he could have British
shipowners *en bloc* for the very least of his sublime messes of
pottage. I am sure it was our shameful lack of national pride in
this direction that led him astray; or so I felt guiltily on the
fourth morning of his stay, when he came ashore at 7 o'clock
and, sitting opposite to me across the breakfast-table, put up his
proposition.

His generous employers, he said, allowed him to spend up to
£40 for pilotage services on entering small ports like Tarawa
and another £40 on leaving. What he had come to get from
me so privately was my signature and an official stamp on a
typewritten document, which, as he spoke, he laid beside my
porridge bowl, flanked by a wad of Treasury notes. The
document assured his employers that he had paid a mythical
Tarawa Port Authority the sum of £80 for inward and out-
ward pilotage services rendered. The wad, containing forty
£1 notes, was my proposed half share of the takings, he cal-
culating to keep the other half for himself.

Beyond doubt, I should have felt suitably outraged by this brazen proposal had Tarawa been a big shipping centre, crammed with wicked sailormen of all nations, where pure minded officials had to keep their eyes skinned for double-crossers round every corner. But this was probably the first white grafter who had ever chanced that bootless way, and being a target for bribery and corruption was an exciting new adventure for me. So I asked him for a start if he expected his £40 to buy anything more than my bare signature.

Well, yes, he admitted, there was just one tiny thing more, and he went on to recall that, on the day of his arrival, a police crew had been out in the district officer's boat marking the spot where his big ship might best lie anchored. Would I please be sure to send the same boat ahead of him before he left that afternoon, this time to mark the deep water passage out of the lagoon. Like that, there would be plenty of visual evidence of pilotage both ways, which he would record in his log, and plenty of his crew could corroborate the entry if ever questions were asked.

But suppose the boat led him wrong and he piled up on the reef? What happened then, was the natural question to ask here.

The boat could never lead him wrong, he replied: he was his own navigator and needed no boats to guide him.

"All right, captain . . . but suppose you yourself make a mistake and then turn round and blame the boat," I suggested—"I'm the one in the soup if you go showing round this document signed by me."

He leaned forward, red in the face: "I am a naffigator, I say, and I am a man of honour," he shouted.

"Of course, of course . . . but this is a dangerous game . . . for me." I pushed the pile of notes into the middle of the table.

He leaned back again. "How much more do you want?" he asked sulkily.

"How much more do you offer?"

128

He hauled a wad from his pocket, silently peeled five one-pound notes from it and added them to mine.

"I want more than that."

Heavily breathing but still wordless, he added another five.

I was somehow certain in that moment that further judicious pressure could wring quite a lot more out of him. I have seldom had a bigger kick out of anything in my life, I must admit. But then my eyes suddenly saw him. Slumped back sweating in a cane chair much too small for his mighty frame, he appeared so helpless, his heavy face, moulded by Nature to look so tough, fallen into puckers of schoolboy mortification. A quick fit of laughter ran away with me and the game was lost. I gathered the fifty notes, together with his egregious document, walked round the table and stuffed them back in his hands.

There was a silence before he spoke. "You mean notting doing?" he asked then, deeply shaken.

"Nothing doing," I repeated. If I had but added, "And now will you kindly get to hell out of my house," the incident would have closed there neatly and with edification for all. But his gloomy looks set me laughing again and, as I returned to my seat, I couldn't resist the temptation to crack a time-worn jest of the islands: "Cheer up, captain! You'll know better next time. No self-respecting man's conscience is worth less than a thousand pounds in these parts."

It made a new man of him. In an instant he was all smiles again. He sprawled his great elbows across the table, his little red eyes leering roguishly into mine. "Ha, ha, ha! Forgiff me, forgiff me!" he chuckled—"Me and my small-time money! I should haff known. Alvays in dese small places it is de same ting. Alvays here is de pig-time money to be found. Ach, you Pritish officials! Alvays for you de pig-time money in de small places!" and guffawing again in generous admiration of our cunning, he invited me heartily to share one last lunch alone with him before he sailed.

I accepted at once, if only because one of his owners'

steaks seemed at the time nothing but a just forfeit for his deplorable cynicism. And I did make a loyal effort, as we gormandized together some hours later, to convert him to a truer, nobler view of my cloth. But all the good that did was to stimulate him to disgraceful stories of all the skulduggeries he had got away with by suborning government officials—and especially Pritish ones like me—up and down the ports of the Far East from 'Yava to Yáppan.' And when I said, self-righteously, "Well, you haven't got away with anything here, anyhow!" he dug me in the ribs: "Ach, you—you great tousand-pound man! Not for notting you stay in dis small place. I vonder . . . I vonder vy you stay here?"

But I'll warrant he never once wondered as hard as I did whenever I thought of my family in England.

Thin Man in the Moonlight

I was always skinny in the Pacific, but never quite so ramshackle as round about that time at Tarawa. The sorcerer's trick up north which had sent me to Betio hospital (he had pulled it off by dropping an infusion of cantharides fly into my daily drink of coconut toddy) had fined me down to under nine stone, and that seemed to leave me simply six feet of skeleton clothed in nothing but skin. The Gilbertese, with their fine, sturdy frames, had a choice of national jokes, quite unprintable here, about thin men and a number of frank words to describe their different appearances. The particular epithet for my type was *kiboriana*, which may be interpreted *buttocks knocked away going under him*. I didn't greatly fancy it at the time, but oh, how I wish it could be honestly said of me now!

It was at this turn of my career that I realized what an advantage stockily-built officers in the colonial service enjoy over thin ones. The stability, the quality of not being easily knocked over, which they command is essential to anyone who

wishes to maintain, come foul, come fair, the true bulldog
look of the old-style British empire builder. I just hadn't got
it: practically everything tripped me up. I often managed to
look far-flung as a result, also bloody, but never by any chance
unbowed.

I was sitting alone, one lovely moonlit evening, on the
lagoon beach of my house at Betio, when a very comely young
man rushed panting from the shadows of the coconut grove
behind me and flung himself on the sand at my feet:
"Save me! Hide me!" he gasped.
Gilbertese men had not the habit of throwing themselves
about like that except in the extremity of terror. There
seemed so little reason for fear of any kind on such a perfect
night; I jumped to a conclusion as he lay struggling for
breath: he was insane, and fancied he had seen some dreadful
demon somewhere among the trees. So I only said, non-
committally, "Where have you come from?"
"From Bairiki," he replied. "Hide me in the calaboose.

Lock us both up. That woman is following us." He laid hold of my ankles: "We have sinned. Lock us up," he kept on pleading.

The village of Bairiki was four miles up-lagoon, across a tidal passage. It seemed, I said to him, a long way for a female demon to be chasing him and his friend, whoever that might be. And anyhow, being locked up in the calaboose might not give him the best protection from so active a spirit; so what about coming along to the hospital with me instead.

He sprang to his feet: "No! No! That woman! She will find us in the hospital and kill us with her akis."

A European axe didn't equate well with a Gilbertese demon. I got up. But, before I could exercise my intelligence further, a high scream rang out from the beach-head and a young woman, naked but for a brief petticoat, came pelting down towards us. "Quick! Quick! The calaboose," she panted: "She comes . . . that woman with her akis!" and hurled herself not, as you might have expected, into the young man's arms, but into mine.

She was small but solid; I, as I have said, tallish but spidery: the impact knocked me flying, clutching at her as I fell. It struck me as the more unfortunate because I was wearing nothing but a loin-cloth myself.

As I rolled bosom to bosom with her on that moonlit strand, my mind worked with unusual speed. This, it told me, must be the other party to the young man's 'both of us'; she, therefore, was the person with whom he had sinned, and the woman chasing them with an axe was his wife. It followed that these intimate gambols which now engaged me were not only in questionable taste for an official grass widower but also, to an unnerving degree, perilous: I had no stomach for demon wives with axes, late at night, in nothing but a loin-cloth. I wrenched myself free, sprang up and bolted for the safeties of my house and a pair of trousers.

They followed hard on my heels, imploring me at the top

of their lungs not to abandon them. I ordered them, with no warmth, to wait on the verandah while I changed.

I felt better buttoned-up in my slacks, but I didn't fancy being involved like this, on behalf of a guilty couple, in a game of hide-and-seek with an outraged wife. However—I thought—there was the situation: if she really was out for murder, locking up this precious pair would be as much for her protection as theirs, while, if she wasn't . . . well . . . they had asked for it. I told them brusquely to follow me and led them in sombre silence through the amethyst glimmer of the coconut grove towards where the twin havens of the male and female lock-ups lay dreaming in the moonlight.

I set the pace at a rapid but stately stride. They crowded in a twittering huddle close up behind me, so engrossed in their fears that neither gave heed to my swinging heels. I don't know whose foot it was that interfered with mine, a hundred yards or so from our gaol, but, male or female, it was all one: my left toe suddenly found itself hooked round my right ankle; my trunk and upper members took an impulsive forward plunge; for the second time that night, I hurtled to the ground. The fact that I hurtled alone on this occasion added little to my pleasure.

I lay face down, saying things into the roadway. Not even a sudden shriek of the girl's deflected my immediate attention to her. It was only when flying feet whipped past my head that I looked up, to see the pair of them racing hand in hand, deadly silent now, towards the prison.

What I felt most, as I sat up, was the need of a little more solitude. I shouldn't have hurried my next move but for the cause of their flight, who now came into my ken. There she was, a female fiend, incredibly massive and bony, charging down on me, chopper in hand, at hurricane speed. She was so close that there wasn't any real hope of getting out of her way; I should have lain down again, quickly; she might have tripped over me then and knocked herself silly. But I panicked and sprang up facing her. She crashed into me; I clung to her

133

resistless bulk; we stood on our heads together for a moment; then I found myself back again at the old game of roly-poly on the ground.

But within three seconds she had flung me off, leapt to her feet and rushed on, chopper aloft, hooting like a siren, in chase of the fugitives. I sprinted after her, my thrice-shaken mind grappling with the new evidence. This demoniac middle-aged Atalanta couldn't possibly be the young man's wife. As for the girl, no angry husband was on her tracks. Therefore, whatever sin the two had sinned, it wasn't the crime I had assumed. I reached this flawless conclusion about thirty yards from the prison gates and six feet behind the huntress's heels, just as her quarry disappeared into the guard-house. Five seconds later, she flew in after them. I caused her to be air-borne myself, with deep pleasure, by cleverly crossing her legs in the last tick of time. There were noises within before she emerged in the grip of two guards.

When at last she gave up fighting for her freedom, we gathered a fact or two from her frothing flood of talk. She was the girl's mother, it seemed. The young couple were soon to be married; the law said they could be; she couldn't stop them; anyhow, it was high time they were, so she said. All that was bad enough, but, even at that, it didn't amount to a matter of life and death. It was when they started spoiling her cook-house that life and death, according to her, came into the picture. She knew what to do about that, nobody better; there wasn't a finer cook in Tarawa; look at her puddings, for example... I could make no sense of it.

"Life and death? Your cook-house?" I only managed to silence her by yelling as loud as I could.

"Yes! My cook-house," she bawled back: "didn't you hear? My cook-house. Four times they have spoiled it. Four times I have changed the place of the earth-oven. And now, tonight, they have poisoned it again."

The whole population of the police lines, male and female, was gathered around now. A groan of sympathy, evidently intended for her, burst from them at her last words. "We hear, we hear," called a woman's voice. "Continue. Make everything clear, for we listen." The men holding her arms dropped them and stood aside.

Placated by this show of fellow-feeling, she began to explain herself more quietly. As every decent housewife knew, she said, love-making was one of the things that the spirits of a Gilbertese earth-oven never could abide. The shame of it soured their stomachs, and the poisonous winds thus engendered inside them were infallibly extruded into every kind of food that came their way for cooking. But these two lovers, being Christian converts, called this nothing but wicked pagan nonsense, and despite her every entreaty, went on and on making assignations in her kitchen.

"Alas, for shame!" wailed a score of horrified, decent pagan matrons, "and what happened then?"

The inevitable thing had happened, she wailed back, bursting into tears. Her husband and aged father, who lived with them, had fallen ill: they were afflicted day and night with the most painful and outrageous flatulence. And, as if that wasn't enough in itself to break any woman's heart, there was their constant ill-temper, which they visited regularly upon herself. That very morning, they had thrashed her between them—taking turns at holding down and beating—until she was nearly dead. What then, she asked us, did we think had been her feelings tonight on finding this pair *at it again*?

Not a mere groan, but a roar of sympathy this time answered her. That was really, for her, the climax of the evening's drama: from then on, every one of us was with her, heart and head, for the pagan purity of her kitchen. There were speeches all round. I contributed a nice piece myself, to which the young man replied with suitable guarantees of amendment. Nobody had the ill-grace to mention the chopper, which lay behind me, where someone had thrown it, quietly winking at the moon. If anyone remembered it, I certainly did not when, at the end, the girl bowed herself before her mother and promised never, never again to enter the kitchen except for cooking. Deeply touched by the generosity of that high surrender and uplifted more than I can say by the pride and honour of my function as father and friend of all of them, I pronounced a short but beautiful little benediction, drew myself up with lifted hand as stately as an archbishop, stepped a pace or two to the rear, thus posed, for my leave-taking, tripped over the chopper, and threw a wild back somersault to the floor.

Unlike my three earlier performances, this one had an appreciative audience. It took a long time to restore decent order by the prisons. And even then, as I limped back alone to my house, I could hear that the three authors of my downfall (trudging homeward now, all happy together) hadn't yet forgotten it. But the moonlight was so wonderful, and peace among men always was worth at least a bruised behind, and somehow I couldn't manage to resent the laughter that came ringing through the trees, first clarion clear, then dwindling to silver bells along the road to Baikiri, and dwindling again until there was no more of it, or them, or anything but sea-whispers and moonbeams in the aching stillness of the night.

Haunted Homes and a Stinking Ghost

There were five European houses scattered through the whispering glades of the palm forest on Betio station in 1923. Two of these had been put up by myself in 1916; the other three were much older; and every one of them, according to the people of Betio village next door, was haunted. The basic trouble was not, I gathered, that they had all happened to be built on pre-haunted ground; there wasn't a foot of soil anywhere up the creeping length of Tarawa that wasn't the lurking place of one fiend or another, and you had to take these as you found them. It was how you dealt with them when you laid out your ground plan and built your house that

really mattered. If you didn't turn on the proper spells—and
how could you if you were a white man?—it followed as a
matter of course that the ghosts or the elementals got in.

One of the two bungalows that I had built had been occupied without delay by an earth-spirit called Na Kun, who
showed himself in the form of a noddy. He croaked "Kun-
kun-kun" at you in the dark of night, and aimed his droppings
at your eye, and blinded you for life if he made a bull's-eye of it.
The other house had a dog on its front verandah: not just a
kamea (that is, a *come-here*) as the white man's dogs were called,
but a *kiri*—one of the breed the ancestors had brought with
them out of the West when, shortly after the creation of the
world by Naareau the Elder, they came to settle on Tarawa.
I could never make out why everyone was so frightened of this
beast. He never *did* anything, simply *was* in the house. For
my own purposes I came to the conclusion that he was like the
mopoke in the celebrated Australian story, so deceptive that
what I occasionally thought I saw on the front verandah and
took to be something else actually was what I took it for,
namely, a mongrel of the old *kiri* strain from the village.

There was a cheerful tale among the villagers that, round
about 1910, an aged friend of mine, a widely loved sorcerer
who dealt in what was called the magic of kindness (meaning
any kind of ritual or charm not intended to hurt anybody)
had posted one of his familiars, the apparition of a grey heron,
on the front verandah of a decrepit bungalow near the hospital. His intent, so the story went, was to get hold of a few
medical secrets for the improvement of his repertoire of
curative potions, especially those which had to do with the
revitalization of flagging manhood. But his constructive plan
was most untimely frustrated when the resident medical officer
was transferred to another house, only just built, but nevertheless already haunted by a hag with two heads. This unpleasant
creature made a most frightful scene when the wizard tried to
take the new premises over for his inquisitive bird. I learned
all these facts from a glorious burlesque show put up for me

one Saturday night by the lads, young and old, of Betio village. The miming of the demon lady's fury, her inhospitable gestures, the rout of the sorcerer, and the total desolation of the heron left all of us, including the venerable gentleman himself, helpless with laughter. But, in the last analysis, behind all the mirth of that roaring crowd, there wasn't a soul present except myself who didn't accept both the familiar and the demon for cold and often terrifying fact.

The oldest house on our station, the one we called the Old Residency, was a pleasant, two-floored structure near the lagoonside haunted by a nameless white beachcomber. This ghost was held in peculiar dread by the villagers, because they regarded it as earthbound for ever, its body having been murdered and left unburied on the beach for the Betio dogs to devour. That kind of revenant was always more *iowawa* (malicious) than any other, everyone believed.

The unhappy man, so the story ran, had been killed on the site of the Residency with a glass bottle by a fellow beachcomber named Tom, a generation or so before the coming of the British flag in 1892, which is to say, somewhere back in the late eighteen-sixties. Nothing else was remembered of him except that he was wearing a sailor's dark shore clothes and thick black boots when he came by his death. Or, at least, that is how his ghost was said to be dressed whenever it allowed itself to be seen about the house.

The villagers talked about him so much and with such conviction that Europeans began to accept the haunt as a fact. It is hard to resist belief in such things when you are lonely and the whole air around you palpitates with horrified credulity. Good Father Guichard of the Sacred Heart Mission, bless him, came down-lagoon fifteen miles when Olivia and I arrived at Tarawa in 1916, especially to warn us against living in the house. But we did live there. We couldn't see why the poor ghost, if it existed, should want to do us any harm. So we had our beds and the baby's cot on the airy gable verandah where he was supposed to walk, clump-clump, in his great thick boots; and all the time we were there we never saw or heard a thing or had the smallest feeling of his unseen presence.

But when I was transferred to the Central Gilberts in 1917 I found a house that gave me quite different sensations. That was the district officer's transit quarters on Tabiteuea, built by George Murdoch, my predecessor in the central islands. It used to stand in a rustling grove of coconut palms by the lagoon beach, a hundred yards or so north of Utiroa village and about the same distance south of the big, whitewashed island prison. It was an airily built, two-roomed shelter of local thatch and timber, a heavenly cool refuge from the ferocious glare of sea and sand beyond the grove. I found it a cheerful place, too, all through the daylight hours, with the talkative Utiroa villagers padding back and forth along the road that passed it to landward.

It changed, though, when darkness fell and the village slept. An uneasiness came upon it then. Or perhaps it was I who changed—I don't know—only I couldn't pass a night there without being haunted by a thought that something was on the edge of happening: something so imminently near, I always felt, that if nothing but one gossamer fold of the darkness could be stripped aside I should see what it was. The idea would come back and back at me as I sat reading or writing. Once or twice, it pulled me up out of sleep, wide awake on the instant, thinking, "Here it is!" But if it was, it never showed itself.

Had this been all, I should never have had the place pulled down. Not even the horrifying odour that visited me there one night would have sufficed of itself to drive me to that extreme. You don't destroy a house built by your predecessor —especially an old stager like George Murdoch—for the sole reason that it was once, for about thirty seconds in your experience, invaded by a smell you couldn't explain. It was what George himself said to me afterwards, when I told him (among other things) how my dog had behaved, that set me looking for another site.

The dog was my terrier, Smith. He was lying in the draught of the roadside doorway one night, while I sat reading. I wasn't deeply absorbed, because I was worried about Anterea, an old friend of mine, who lay ill in the village—so ill I was sure he wouldn't last the night. Perhaps that made me particularly susceptible to whatever it was. Anyhow, I felt myself suddenly gripped as I sat by a more than usually disturbing sense of that imminent something. It had never had any particular direction before, but now it seemed to impend from the roadway. I was aware, also, of having to fight a definite dread of it this time instead of greeting it with a kind of incredulous expectancy. I sprang up, staring nervously out into the dark beyond the door. And then I noticed Smith. Hackles bristling, gums bared, he was backing step by step away from the door, whimpering and trembling as he backed.

"Smith!" I called. He gave me one quick piteous look, turned tail and bolted, yelping as if I had kicked him, through the seaward door. I heard him begin to howl on the beach just as that unspeakable odour came sweeping into the room, wave upon wave of the breath of all corruption, from the road.

Plain anger seized me as I stood. That was natural, I think. I had made myself a fine figure of fun for whoever was outside, leaping to my feet and goggling like a scared rabbit through the doorway, a glorious butt for this nasty trick. It hurt. I forgot Smith and dashed out into the road. But there wasn't a clue for eye, or ear, or nose in the hissing darkness under the wind-blown palms. I found nobody and nothing until my running feet brought me to the fringe of Utiroa village; and there I heard a sound that stripped me of all my anger. It was the noise of women wailing and men chanting, mixed with the rhythmic thud-thud of heavy staves on the ground. I couldn't mistake it. A Gilbertese *bomaki* ceremony was in full swing; some villager's departing soul was being ritually sped on its difficult road from earth to paradise. I knew then that my old friend Anterea had not lasted the night, and I lost all heart for my silly chase.

There was no taint on the air of the house when I got back. I fell asleep untroubled by anything but my own sadness. But Smith stayed out on the beach, and I couldn't persuade him to remain indoors after dark for the few more days I spent on Tabiteuea.

The rest of the story is George Murdoch's. He had settled down to trading on Kuria Island after his retirement from the administrative service, so I took the next chance I could of running across to tell him of my feelings about the house, and Smith's queer behaviour, and the foetid smell someone had put across me.

"So he's been making friends with you, has he?" said George reflectively when I had finished, and, instead of answering when I asked who "he" might be, he went on, "From about the middle of Utiroa village to a bit north of the prison—that's his beat. Aye, he's a stinking old nuisance. But, mind you, there's no real harm in him."

'He,' in short, according to George, was an absurd ghost known to the villagers as *Tewaiteaina*, or One Leg, whose habit for several centuries it had been to walk—or, rather, hop—that particular stretch of Tabiteuea, every night of the year without exception, scaring everybody stiff who saw him go by. George spoke of him with a sort of affectionate irritation, as if he really existed. It was too ridiculous.

"But, Mr. Murdoch," I interrupted, "there's a ghost for every yard of the Gilberts if you swallow all that village stuff!"

He eyed me humorously: "But there's only one ghost who stinks, young fella-me-lad, and that's old One Leg. Not that he plays that trick often, mind you. Just sometimes, for friendship's sake. Now, if you'll stop interrupting, I'll tell you . . .

"I'd heard nothing about him when I had the prison and the rest house built where they are," he went on, "otherwise I might have chosen somewhere else. Or I might not. What's the odds, anyway? The creature's harmless. So there I was one dark, still night, with a prison nicely full of grand, strong lads up the road and myself sitting all serene in the rest house, enjoying a page or two of the King's Regulations. I say I was all serene, you'll note. The house had stood three years, and I'd never been troubled by the Something's-Going-To-Happen notion you've made such a point of. Sheer nonsense, that, I'm telling you straight!"

"Yes, Mr. Murdoch," I said humbly.

"Well, you'll grow out of it, I suppose," he comforted me. "So there I sat, a grown man, with not one childish fancy to make a fool of me, when in from the roadway crashed that stinking thing and hit me like a wall. Solid. A fearful stench. You were right about that. Corruption and essence of corruption from the heart of all rottenness—that's what I said to myself as I fought my way through it to the door . . . How did I know it came from the road, you say? What does that matter—I *did* know; so don't interrupt with your questions.

"I'll admit the uncanny suddenness of it gave me the shudders at first. But I was angry, like you, by the time I reached the road. I thought some son-of-a-gun was taking a rise out of me. So I dashed back into the house, snatched up a hurricane lamp and started running hell for leather towards the prison. The reek was as thick as a fog that way, and I followed my nose.

"I hadn't gone far, though, before I heard a patter and a rush from ahead, and a great ox of a prison guard came charging full-tilt out of the darkness and threw himself at me, gibbering like a cockatoo. As I struggled out of his clutches, I caught something about someone called One Leg who'd gone hop-hopping past him into the prison yard. Well . . . there was my clue. 'Is it One Leg that raised this stink?' I shouted. 'Yes,' he screamed back. 'One Leg . . . the ghost!' I only stayed to call him a blanky fool and belted on.

"But I wasn't quick enough to catch up with the trouble.

142

When I got near the prison yard, something else had started. The whole crowd inside the men's lock-up had gone mad . . . raving mad . . . yelling their heads off . . . and the noise of them flinging themselves against the door was like thunder. I knew the padlock wouldn't last if that went on: I heard it crack like a pistol as I came up to the yard entrance; and, begum, before you could say knife, I was down under the feet of a maniac mob stampeding out into the bush.

"I picked myself up and made a bee-line for the lock-up; ran half-way down the gangway between the beds, swinging my lamp around; found not a soul there; charged out again to Anterea's house in the corner of the yard . . . why, what's the matter now?"

I had sat bolt upright and exclaimed, "Anterea?" When I repeated it, he said, "Yes, the head warder. Retired before your time, but he's still going strong in Utiroa. One of the few who never gave a damn for old One Leg. Would you believe it? He was sleeping like a baby when I got to him. Hadn't heard a sound and said he couldn't smell a thing, though the place was still humming fit to knock you down. But he got going quick enough when I told him the news. He and I hunted the bush for those poor idiots till the crack of dawn. They came in willingly enough at sun-up—all but Arikitaua, that's to say—and we had a fine pow-wow together round Anterea's shack, waiting for him to turn up. That's when I got all the dope about One Leg.

"They'd all seen him hopping up the gangway between the beds, so they claimed. There wasn't a light, but they'd seen him. 'Fiddle!' I said to that and Anterea backed me. So, just for the hell of it, I turned on him then, and asked him what of the smell I'd smelt and he hadn't; and immediately about half of them butted in to say they hadn't smelt it either; and, by the same token, the other half had. It was all very puzzling until somebody explained that One Leg only brought his saintly odour along for the particular friends of the deceased, and then, of course, it was as clear as mud. Which

143

deceased? I wanted to know. 'Oh, anyone who dies within the limits of his beat,' says my clever friend—'he turns it on as soon as the soul has left the body.'

"You could have knocked me down with a feather if there had been a corpse in sight. But there wasn't. So I said a few wise words and left them to think up another story. I had a mind to go and enquire in the village after our missing number, Arikitaua . . . an Utiroa man . . . I liked him a lot. But I hadn't gone fifty steps when a new hullaballoo from the lock-up stopped me in my tracks. I thought they were starting another One Leg stunt. But it was only poor Arikitaua this time. Yes . . . there he was—rolled off his bed on the floor up against the far end wall—where my lamp hadn't reached him . . . quite dead. I reckon it was just heart disease."

We sat silent a long time; then George said reflectively, "What with this and that, I'm surprised you didn't hear of a friend's death in Utiroa after the old stinker put it across you."

I told him then of Anterea.

"Well . . . well . . . think of that now," said George. ". . . and Anterea an unbeliever. Kind of friendly, I call it. There never was any real harm in old One Leg."

He was furious when I had a new rest house built on the other side of the island—as furious as a man might be who has led you up the garden path to his own confusion. But he never would admit he'd been pulling my leg. And then again, what was it that scared my dog so?

Rum Revenge

There was another story I got at that time from George Murdoch: for I took every opportunity of getting him to tell me about his early days in the islands. It was not a ghost story this time—for, from what George told me, there was nothing intangible about Tem Binoka. He recounted the incident with what seemed to me considerable relish, perhaps because in a way, he felt it showed with what respect the Gilbertese first received the white man's law.

Tem Binoka, High Chief of Abemama, Kuria and Aranuka, had a weakness for revenge. It expressed itself in his approach to the biting of eyeballs. An ordinary Gilbert Islander of those days would merely kill his man in battle, pluck out an eyeball on the spot, bite it in two, and go his way content. It was a public gesture—the right thing to do—and that was the end of it. But Binoka was different. He did not seek the publicity of battles; he had executioners enough to see that men lost their heads secretly whenever he whispered; he craved nothing but to revel ritually and alone in the ignominy of the dead. Their heads were rolled at his feet on a dais. Sometimes he was not in the mood to attend to the eyeballs at once. In that event, the heads were preserved until he was. He knew how to preserve them.

Terror and death reigned with him over Abemama, Kuria and Aranuka until 1892. But then Captain H. M. Davies, R.N., appeared in H.M.S. *Royalist* to declare a British Protectorate over the Gilbert Islands. The first man the captain looked for on Abemama was George McGhee Murdoch. George was trading there at the time for copra and shark-fins.

A code of native laws, which George himself had helped to frame, was set up by Captain Davies. All that matters about it here is that it was quite inelastic about homicide. It made no allowance at all for the customary right of a High Chief to destroy his subjects at discretion. Binoka was told that he could henceforward count with confidence upon being hanged for the murder of even the meanest of his underlings.

Binoka did not argue: there was a shrewd brain in that gorged mountain of fat. He asked instead, with realism, what price he would now be required to pay for his past errors. No price, he was told. The new law was not retroactive. It would begin to run the next morning, from the hour of hoisting the Flag and reading the Queen's Proclamation. His jowl began to shake with silent laughter as he waddled out. George always reproached himself for disregarding that strange mirth.

A year or two later, Captain Davies was back again in Abemama. He came this time as a hydrographer, to chart the approaches to the lagoon. He found George now officially presiding as Government Agent and Tax-Collector, and Binoka behaving himself as High Chief with almost piteous constitutionality. With George's help, a naval survey party was based on an islet by the lagoon entrance; and there Binoka provided, for the especial comfort of officers, an exquisitely thatched dwelling-house near the beach. His little speech of presentation was touching, George said. And he capped everything by asking the captain to accept as a further gift a small keg of rum which he had brought along with him.

Binoka's rum was, of course, a byword in the Pacific. The New Bedford whalers had taught him the trick of maturing it with raw meat and charcoal. It was his personal discovery that chunks of red porpoise-flesh did every bit as well as the white man's beef. So it was very natural, after all, for Captain Davies to jump at the offer.

It was one of those brass-bound, two-gallon kegs complete with tap. The tap gave some difficulty, but they managed to draw off a bottleful there and then. According to George, it was a triumphant liquor. It rolled around his gums, he said, as soft as mother's milk. I dare say it did. Binoka's gross body shook with mirth as he drank with them. He had a high falsetto giggle, like a girl's. The captain did not like it until George explained it was his native courtesy. They finished the bottle between them.

George returned to the camp a few evenings later. The navigating lieutenant had joined the captain there. Opinion about the quality of the rum still ran heavens high, but the tap had been giving more and more trouble. The thing merely dripped when they turned it on. George tried it: "Well," he said at last, "why not unship and clean it? There might be a bit of porpoise meat stuck in it." They did so. But it was not meat they found. It was human hair. And that, as George put it to me, looked rather queer to everyone. So they investigated further, and found inside the keg the thing that accounted for the rum's rare bouquet. It was a pickled human head.

Binoka proved beyond a shadow of doubt that the man had been decapitated before the hoisting of the Flag—the evening before: just after Captain Davies had so kindly promised that the law would not be retroactive. That point being clear, what about the head? His habit from of old had been to preserve all these heads of enemies together in a single barrel. They were withdrawn as needed for the ceremonial biting of eyeballs. This one had somehow got itself isolated. Must he suffer for that? There was surely nothing in the new law to forbid the peaceful ritual. Would the captain therefore, please, restore the valued relic at once? Had not the gift of the rum in itself been generous enough?

But at that point he broke down. The fullness of his revenge suddenly overwhelmed him. A high ripple of giggles burst from his monstrous flesh. He staggered round the floor before them, racked and sobbing, and drunk with laughter. It was ghastly beyond words, George said. They sat mutely waiting for him to recover himself. When at last he did, he wiped his streaming eyes, spat on the floor, and lurched from the room without another word.

8

Timely Arrival

At this point of imperial history, no such luxury was known in the Western Pacific High Commission services as passage grants for grass widows like Olivia who wanted to visit their husbands in the field. But Olivia inherited that small legacy in 1923 and splashed the lot on a visit to the Gilbert Islands when I had been six or seven months at Tarawa. She reached me, alas, only to find our station plunged in sadness. A month before her arrival, pneumonia had robbed our new cadet-in-training—young Scooter, as all of us called him—of his adored little son.

The blow had been the more bitter for Scooter because, on the night the little boy died, our senior medical officer Kitson, the only doctor there, who was himself to die of Bright's disease only a few weeks later, had been too sick to leave his bed. Even if he could have been aroused from his semi-comatose state, he could have done no more to save the child's life on that night of crisis than, for the last week, he had been courageously battling to do. The sulpha drugs and penicillin were as yet unknown to medical science, and Betio hospital did not run to oxygen tents.

But neither Scooter nor his wife could ever after be persuaded that Kitson had not been, through wanton neglect, the killer of their son. The hate and despair they nursed defied all consolation, and seemed to flow from them through the station like some dark river, while Kitson, sick beyond hope of cure, lay in his house waiting for death to take him.

It was a tremendous relief when, out of the blue, the Fiji government's motor yacht *Pioneer* broke in upon us. The *Pioneer* was a comfortable little craft of perhaps 400 tons— the ex-playboat of an American millionaire—which our High Commission territories had helped to purchase and were glad to get on occasional loan for local purposes. She had come now to take me on a tour of the colony instead of Reggie McClure. Reggie, for health reasons, had had to take vacation leave rather suddenly and I was to carry on for him until his return.

So we were able to get our poor Kitson across to Ocean Island at once, where he could lie in a good hospital with kind Dr. Gould and a trained nurse to attend him, while Olivia, instead of coming on tour with me, stood by to make a home at the residency for his grief-stricken wife.

Empire Bunk

The trip round in the *Pioneer* that followed has always remained memorable to me because it brought me into contact with Dr. Samuel H. Lambert. That great American friend and helper of Britain was stationed in those days at Suva, Fiji, as representative of the Rockefeller Foundation. To his labours there are due prime thanks for the princely grants of money poured by his Foundation into aid for all the Western Pacific

High Commission medical services. The *Pioneer* had now brought him our way to carry out a survey of the incidence of hookworm in the Gilbert and Ellice Groups.

We had known Lambert for the selfless worker he was long before we saw him among us. We had also heard a few tales about him: he was the sort of character around whom stories have a habit of gathering, like jackdaws round a belfry. His way with pretentious humbugs was particularly well documented. One report related (I can't possibly say how truly) that, having landed on a certain British island to do a job of work with the medical authorities, he was bailed up by X—, a very senior administrative official noted for his pomposity, and deflected from the hospital into a walking tour of the main settlement. He bore the interruption with courteous patience until he realized that he was being used merely as an audience for a peripatetic lecture on the 'awful lot' Americans didn't know, and the British did, about colonial administration. Even then, he only insisted politely on being guided without further delay to the hospital, and that would have been the end of it if the disgruntled X— had not snapped crossly as they parted, "You might at least say what you think of our little capital, doctor!"

"Your little capital? Ah . . . yes . . ." replied Lambert, stroking his chin thoughtfully, "well . . . the way things are . . . it looks to me as if all it needs to put it right is one helluva dose of American ignorance about colonial administration. That's what I'm here right now to see about, if you'll excuse me," and he disappeared into the hospital.

It was part of my business on tour to take him and his staff of Fijian microscopists into the big government meeting house at each island we visited and introduce them to the assembled people. Those preliminaries completed, they would leave for the half-dozen thatched huts above the weather beach that we called an 'island hospital' and, helped there by the dresser in charge, get along with their hookworm survey while I went on with my own work in the meeting house.

But at Vaitupu in the Ellice Group Lambert stayed on with me for some reason I have forgotten, and so heard a message of thanks which, through an interpreter, I was conveying to the people by request of the Secretary of State for the Colonies. With the regal generosity of their race, the Vaitupuans had clubbed together to give a great slice of their richest land—nearly twenty acres, if I remember right—for the support of a small secondary school for the Ellice group that we were starting there.

But in 1923 one didn't talk to the islanders about official thanks from such an abstraction as a Secretary of State. They knew what district officers were; they recognized the Old Man of Ocean Island; they even managed to grasp the idea of an aged potentate far away in Fiji called the Ai-Kamitina. But above and beyond that remote elevation of the High Commissioner they could imagine no chief save a royal one; and if they gave gifts to help the King's local government, their simple hearts took it for granted that they were earning the King's personal gratitude.

So, as a matter of course, I returned thanks to Vaitupu that day in King George's name, not the Secretary of State's. It was so entirely natural to do so that, as I spoke, it didn't even strike me a newcomer might find it strange. Lambert's reply to my first remark when the meeting ended therefore came as quite a poke in the eye.

"Wasn't that a wonderful gift of land for the school, doctor!" I exclaimed as we walked out of the *maneaba*: "It's going to save hundreds of pounds a year on the ration account."

"Wonderful . . . wonderful," he agreed—"and oh, boy, your speech about it! You sure can pull that Empire bunk over these people to perfection."

Well, there you are. In his eyes—and there were none more honest in the Pacific—I had been playing a deceitful little imperialist game, stringing along a bunch of simple, generous folk with bogus talk of kings and their gratitude. For

my part, I had used the King's name simply and without guile, as a symbol of Britain which everyone could understand, instead of an official title which would have been meaningless to everyone. Beyond that, the symbol was one which, for many field officers of my day in the Pacific, stood for nothing so little as the idea of white sovereignty or brown subjection, and for nothing so much as an ideal of fellow-service along a common road. If there was in fact anyone out there who clung to the notion of a kingly overlord and father, whose word was law—and rightly so—for half creation, it was the Gilbertese and Ellice villagers themselves. Those, not we, were the truly intransigent imperialists in that part of the world.

This Happy Breed of Men

I am sure King George V would have been surprised at the number of poor relations he had among our government staff in the islands. It wasn't that any of us ever, to my knowledge, had presumption enough to claim for himself even the remotest degree of consanguinity with the Sovereign. The idea came from our parishioners. These looked at things from the basic assumption that a great chief would naturally want all the jobs everywhere for his own flesh and blood. If he hadn't that amount of family love in his heart, he couldn't conceivably be a great chief, they said. So, inasmuch as King George *was* a great chief, particularly well known for the example of family love he set, it followed that every one of us, whatever his rank in the local service, had to be either a blood relation of his or at least one of his in-laws.

The courteous hypothesis about a new officer always allowed him the higher of these degrees, i.e., the blood royal, for a start. But from then on, the correctness of the assumption was strictly under test. If in fact it was incorrect, the

L

truth would surely out, for the breed could not but tell, said the islanders. In other words, kingly was as kingly did; or, even better, kingly was as kingly didn't, because the virtues attributed to royalty seemed always to be expressed as avoidances. Not to be a physical coward; not to boast, not to shout when annoyed; not to be pompous, or *unun* (addicted to anger), or *tiritiri* (quick to violence) with anyone, or parsimonious to family, or discourteous to dependents: this ideal list of royal negatives was written down for me by Airam Teeko of Abemama, a chief of the house of that redoubtable Tem Binoka, whom R. L. Stevenson made famous in the late eighties.

It was a modest enough standard to live up to; furthermore, I don't think it was ever very straitly applied to any of us. The amazing affection of the islanders for our race wanted every one of us to prove royal if possible. But there had to be now and then a throw-out. The King's blood could not be insulted by retaining really dyed-in-the-wool boasters or shouters, for example, on the panel of his putative kinsmen. So these were relegated in due course to the panel of his in-laws, and he was respectfully commiserated for having had such unfortunate alliances foisted upon him; or, as in very bad cases like Albert's down at Arorae, they were declared to be *rang*, or baseborn pretenders, and dismissed from memory, never to be named again.

The Imperialist

The friend who revealed these truths to me, Airam Teeko, chief of the royal house of Abemama and Native Magistrate of his island, was a lumbering six-foot albino who had had to contend all his life with the handicap of a revolting ugliness. A lesser man than he would have been early embittered by the shrinking of all children from his terrible looks added to the pain of mortally sensitive eyes and skin, forever

154

unable to support the equator's blistering sun. But behind that tortured exterior there lay a spirit as patient and serene as any I have ever met. He was the kind of man one sought out first when things went wrong, because of the silent peace that was in him. Beyond that, too, though he knew no English and had enjoyed no education above the level of his local primary school, he had the natural lucidity of thought and speech that goes with high intellect. I never ceased to be astonished at the way that delving mind of his rooted out the essentials of any subject, however unfamiliar its details.

Airam was one of the very few islanders of his generation (he had passed fifty in 1917, when I was district officer at Abemama) to whom I ever ventured to reveal the horrid truth about the Secretary of State for the Colonies. It shocked him deeply at first that any such individual should have managed to obtrude himself so insolently between the King-Emperor and his Empire. I had to take him through quite a lot of Anson (whose volumes I had cherished from Cambridge days) before he was reasonably comfortable about the element called the Crown in a constitutional monarchy. And when I spoke of a Secretary of State who came and went according to the fortunes of his political party, and of permanent officials who stayed on whatever happened to him, he was especially perplexed.

"Who then among these three, Kurimbo—the King, the Sekeriteri who comes and goes, and the menials under the Sekeriteri who remain forever sitting and writing—who among these is our real master?" he asked me one day, as innocent as a new Candide groping his way to truth through the white man's endless illogicalities.

The only true answer in terms of purely material control would of course have been, "None of these is our real master, for above them all a far more powerful overlord, the United Kingdom Treasury, is permanent cock of the colonial walk." But that would have meant a further series of excursions, which might have broken his heart, down the blinder alleys of Whitehall imperialism. I answered instead with the mystical truth, very much more vital to our service in those days than the material one, that the King was our ultimate master. As his official Pangloss, I could not in any case have said anything to leave him better convinced for the moment that all was for the best in the best of possible empires.

Nevertheless, from that time on he was constant in his enquiries about our system. He would spend hours devising lists of questions and writing them down on the left-hand pages of little black exercise books, so that my answers could be recorded on the right. His favourite way of approaching a discussion was to throw out some experimental positive conjecture for a starter and wait for my reaction.

Sitting on my guest mat one evening not long after we had agreed on the Sovereign for our chief, he suddenly said, "How rich that King must be: for see how many servants like you he sends across the seas and pays to represent him!"

I could hardly leave it at that, could I? He had to learn something nearer to the truth some time or other; so I said flatly, somehow hating myself for the admission, "It isn't the King who pays us, Airam."

"But how can that be, since it is he who appoints you to work for him?"

"It is not the King who appoints us: his servants in the Colonial Office do that."

"You mean the Sekeriteri-men who come and go?"

"No, I mean the sit-sit-men who remain and write."

"What? That crowd. Are those then the men who hold all the money, and measure out your wages, and pay to bring you here and pay again to send you away from us whenever they like to other lands?"

"Those indeed are the men who fix my wages, and send me now here, now there, without asking either you or me about it. But they haven't any money and it isn't they who do the paying."

"Then is it the good, the generous chiefs and people of Buritan who pay you to look after us? And is it for these that the sit-sit writers work?"

"Well, I suppose it is true that the Colonial Office works for the good taxpayers of Britain; but the good taxpayers of Britain would simply hate the idea of paying for a single thing I am doing in or for the Gilbert Islands!"

"Alas, Kurimbo!" he exclaimed at that, "my thought has reached its end. In Heaven's name now say yourself who it is that does the paying."

"Why, *you* do, Airan—you, and your people, and the companies, and the traders from whom we collect taxes in this country of yours."

"But the copra tax that we give every year to the government is our tribute to King Tioti [George]," he protested gravely. "Are you telling me now that it is not sent to him in London?"

"It is not sent. He would not wish it. He is grateful for the generosity of his people, but he has enough of his own money to live on."

"So the tribute we give him is spent here, by his order, for our benefit."

"It certainly is spent on local services, and I am quite sure the King would wish for nothing else."

"Therefore, in the end, it is indeed the King who pays you to look after us," he finished triumphantly, and I found in myself no wish to rob him of his dialectic victory.

When we talked together after that of how the colony's little jigsaw puzzle of a budget was put together, without a penny's help from Britain, I was often afraid his fine faith in our imperial generosity might one day be shaken. But it never was. He never tired of reminding me of that freely returned royal 'tribute.' And if ever, in the dark of the night before dawn, private doubts about the purity of Whitehall's motives did assail him, his inborn urge to serve his own people was so royally strong I'm sure that, like Candide, he found the best answer to every uncertainty in the end was to cut the cackle and get along, when morning broke, with another little job of work in the local garden.

9

Mistaken Policy

It was early in 1925 that the *Pioneer* finally dropped me at
Ocean Island and returned with Lambert to Fiji. Those were
the difficult days before we had the Chinese and Gilbertese
labourers living and working in areas well apart from each
other. The Gilbertese were housed in a location immediately
above a small railway line used for the transport of phosphate;
the Chinese location lay immediately below it. At one point,
nothing but the breadth of the permanent way and a public
footpath—less than fifty paces in all—divided the lower
boundary of the one from the upper boundary of the other.
That was not nearly enough for peace of mind between
races of men who withdrew from each other every evening
savage from having had to work cheek by jowl throughout
the day.

The policy of bundling irreconcilables like the Chinese

and Gilbertese hugger-mugger together in mining field and workshop was as cruel as it was dangerous. For an oriental, deeply sensitive to losses of physical dignity, the schoolboy horseplay of the islanders—the upsetting of his wheelbarrow, the spilling of his paint pot, the jogging of his elbow, the uproarious barging around—made something like a nightmare of his working day. To an islander, incapable of imagining a shame more horrible than incest, the stock Chinese retort about his relations with his grandmother (which he had learned to recognize by the sound of it) was an insult that screamed for blood-letting. There was constant friction between yellow and brown. It was madness, in the face of all the facts, to keep the two races housed side by side without even enclosing fences to prevent them from prowling around each other's locations at night.

Although, in all other respects, the British Phosphate Commissioners were notably thoughtful employers, they had to pay heavily for that one big standing mistake. It kept the Chinese in such a constant state of nervous tension that they were ready to lay down tools on the slightest provocation. The reason for one memorable strike was the non-arrival from Hong Kong of a consignment of tinned lily shoots. The ration scale in the contract of employment said lily shoots twice a week; so, when the stock ran out, eight hundred coolies sat down and remained sitting until the delayed supply arrived.

In those days, the duty of settling strikes usually fell to the resident commissioner. The Gilbertese labourers expected his intervention as of right when they had a grievance, and about 50 per cent of the Chinese coolies tolerated it amiably enough as a guarantee that the administration was interested in their side of affairs as well as the employer's. On the other hand there were always plenty who distrusted official meddling altogether, and attended our meetings with strikers only to guess aloud at uncomfortable moments how much the B.P.C. paid us for cheating them back to work.

Reggie McClure, humorous, kind and never at a loss for
an answer, showed superb technique in dealing with this sort
of sabotage. He replied once that the reward offered to him
personally for cheating them in any way at all was £1,000.
"But," he added, "as you are much too clever to be deceived
by any trick of mine, I have never pocketed a penny up to
date." Every face in his audience was illuminated with
instant delight at this extraordinarily courteous tribute to their
superior cunning. They plainly thought it worth a thousand-
pound response, for they returned to work the next morning
without further parley.

But anxious times came for all of us when they hit on the
device of striking work in order to secure attention to their
grievances against the police. Not that they ever brought
a charge against an innocent man; they had no need to do
that, for, although our Ellice Islanders and Fijians could be
trained to the patient perfection of London's own metro-
politan force, our Gilbertese—alas!—had not their marvellous
restraint under provocation, and too often manhandled
abusive coolies. But it did seem rather unfair that their impatience should be visited upon the pocket of the wretched
employer, however blind his labour policy.

Reggie McClure used to say, looking at things from the
angle of the local manager, that not even an archangel would
have liked to have eight hundred coolies sitting down on him
idle for as long as it took the O/C police to go into the charges
against his constables. To which Stuartson Methven would
reply that not even an archangel trying his best to get at the
truth of things would have liked to have the blanky manager
breathing down the back of his neck until he found it.

Thus completely did those poor, illiterate, helpless victims
of imperial exploitation, the coolies, contrive to range their
exploiter on their own side against the government and then
to split the government party into two contending factions.
I personally failed so often to satisfy them as an arbitrator, or
to understand the hidden ways of their thought, or to get

them within a mile of understanding what I liked to regard as my open ways, that I came at last to believe there could be no possible bridge of shared sentiment over which they and I might ever approach one another across the abyss of our mutual ignorances. Yet, in the long run, it was the generous sensitiveness of their response to a purely private gesture of mine that settled the most serious anti-police strike I ever had to face.

A Gift of Crackers

It happened soon after the *Pioneer* had brought me back to Ocean Island. It never would have happened, I'm sure, if Stuartson Methven had still been O/C police and prisons there. But he had lately been sent as district officer to Fanning and Washington Islands, 1,600 miles to eastwards of the

Gilberts, and I was under orders to hold down his job at Head-quarters as well as Reggie's until further notice.

That was in itself a dangerous arrangement. With all the racial tension there was, I should have been wise to forget for the moment that I was acting resident commissioner and give all my time to police and prisons. But I tried to do both jobs and saw my mistake only too late, when Sergeant-Major Taitusi came to report the madness of Corporal Teakai.

Teakai was at that time the sole Gilbertese N.C.O. in the police force, the rest being Fijians and Ellice Islanders. Through all his eleven years of service he had a name for gentleness. It was because of his known patience that we put him and nobody else in charge of Chinese prisoners, working parties. Yet Sergeant-Major Taitusi had caught him flogging one poor, weedy little coolie before him up the precipitous bush track that led from the beach to the prison yard. His weapon was a tarred rope-end; his victim had a heavy load of sand hoisted on his shoulder. Taitusi sprang forward to snatch the rope from Teakai's hand. Teakai resisted. In the tussle that followed, the prisoner quietly dropped his load to the ground and slipped away into the dense bush. The sun set twenty minutes later. We searched in vain for the missing man through the whole of the following week.

During that time, Teakai stood his trial. There could be no defence for what he had done, but Chinese witnesses proved beyond doubt that it was his only offence of the kind. Also, he was the only man in the colony who held a medal for life-saving from the Royal Humane Society.

I felt too small a man myself to decide out of hand that these things, together with all his years of perfect service, should be passed over as though they had never been because of that single hour's madness that had seized him on the hill-side. So I gave him his own choice between dismissal with three months' imprisonment on one hand and reduction to the third grade of constable with a flogging from his sergeant-major on the other. He choose the second and, next morning, took his punishment with fortitude and dignity from Taitusi. We were able to get him transferred to the Gilbert Group within the next few days. He never returned to Ocean Island.

Three days after he was gone, we found the escaped prisoner. He had been hiding in the desolation of a dug-out mining area, a wilderness of blazing rocks where never a blade of green could grow for cover from the sun's blistering glare. Things had gone fairly easily for him at first, nevertheless, for he had been able to feed with his friends at night in the Chinese location, and stay hidden with them until the dark before dawn. But on the third or fourth morning, scrambling down steep crags back into his hiding-place, he had had a fall which, though it broke no bones, so terribly bruised and wrenched his frail body that he could no longer walk. He had lain trapped and starving and flayed raw in the furnace heat of that inferno for five days before our search patrols found him. His bruises were found to have gone gangrenous when he was brought to hospital. He died a day or two later.

His death was the signal for an instant strike by the Chinese labourers. A deputation told the manager that they would remain out until repatriated unless the government agreed to their terms. The terms were that the whole police force, as a gesture of contrition for what they called Teakai's murder of their comrade, should follow the dead man's body to the graveside with uniforms stripped of buttons, badges, stripes, or any other kind of distinguishing mark.

The manager referred this ultimatum to me. His note arrived just as all the strikers came streaming up the hillside to surround our lonely office, and as our Chinese interpreter put it, "to plead aloud for reasonable conference with some honourable representative of the government."

As I looked over the verandah rail at that yelling mob, it came to me that, whatever else might happen, this must be the end of my official career. A man was dead who would have been alive but for his escape from prison—who would never have wanted to escape but for the savagery of a policeman—who could not have suffered that savagery had I, the man in charge, been a hundred per cent on my job. Yet, responsible as the government had become through me, there could be no question of accepting either their mistaken charge of murder or their half-malicious, half-piteous plan to humiliate the police. Not even the ghost of a compromise on those two points was possible, and, as surely as I ruled them out of court, the strike would be on. There would probably be riots, too, judging from the temper of the crowd already.

There was a boulder-strewn space over-arched by coconut palms on the hillside below the office. While the interpreter invited them to meet me there, I walked down to a shaded rock a little higher than the rest. They let me through in silence, but making only just enough room for passageway. I shall remember until I die the acrid reek of phosphate dust and sweat that closed around me in those moments. All the crude toil and poverty of their lives seemed summed up in it. I was wrung with a sudden, shamed sense of the gross handicaps they suffered, the cushioned ease of my own lot. It did nothing to lighten my feeling of personal guilt towards them and the dead man as I waited for everyone to find seats.

They said their say quietly to begin with; but it was hopeless from the start; since leaving the manager, their committee had stiffened the terms: in addition to the humiliation of the police, they now required the recall of Teakai from Tarawa and his trial for murder. We argued round that single point quite uselessly for two hours, I doing nothing but explain why I couldn't agree, they retorting with ever-mounting clamour that nothing but a murder trial would satisfy them. We had not even began on the matter of the funeral when a wild fellow whom we called Peter the Painter leapt from his seat, yelled at the rest to follow him and started to walk off. They were all on their feet together then, screaming at the interpreter with brandished fists.

"Sir," he said to me, his voice bland, his manner unperturbed, "this would seem to be a serious emergency. The saying of something of a highly constructive kind at once is indicated, if it happens to occur to Your Honour," and, without pausing for an answer, he raised his voice to a siren screech, bidding them be reseated.

They obeyed him.

I hadn't a word more to say about their terms. I was sick to death of the argument. My mind was already resigned to the strike and its consequences, whatever they might be. The only thing I did want to say was something entirely personal. It was that, strike or no strike, I was as grieved as they were at the death of their friend, because I felt that my negligence had indirectly led to it. Though I couldn't, as head of the government, do as they demanded, I could at least make a private grief-offering of all the fireworks they thought necessary for a happy funeral, if they would allow me to do so.

I did know how much they valued fire-crackers at burials; but the idea of bribing them back to work with such an offer was so far from my mind that I got up to leave as soon as the interpreter had finished talking. I wasn't surprised when the whole crowd sprang up, with renewed clamour. They were evidently yelling their contempt of me and my crackers. "No wonder!" I thought, sick at heart. "It must have sounded pretty cheap to them."

I had turned on my heel to get out when a bunch of them, headed by Peter the Painter, surged forward through the shouting mob. It looked like instant trouble. "What now?" I asked the interpreter, turning back to stand my ground as shakily as you like to imagine. In the same second, Peter the Painter stopped ten feet short of me, screamed a few words through the din with his arm raised high as if to strike, then suddenly swerved left and led the whole seven hundred of them, except for two men, at a gallop down the hillside.

The interpreter turned to me in a convulsion of high-pitched, expressionless sniggers. "The organizing committee paused before leaving to tell you your face is like a looking-glass," he explained when he could manage to speak.

I had expected some sort of insult, but definitely not this contemptuous comment on my looks, topped off with his shameless, open amusement. "And you dare to stand there giggling while they march off to play hell in the settlement!" I began. "Why you . . ."

But he let me go no further. "Excuse . . . excuse! No hell whatever in settlement. My giggles the laughter of congratulation. 'Looking-glass face' high expression of Chinese esteem. Courteous gift of crackers-money is graciously accepted; these two men are waiting to receive same from your hands."

They returned to work the same day. There was not another anti-police strike on Ocean Island while Peter the Painter remained there.

Spirited Encounter

When the average Gilbertese villager of thirty years ago came to while away a few months in prison, his main idea as a rule was to settle down to a lovely, long, well-fed rest from the grim task of food-getting for his family. No such insults to his intelligence as *chevaux de frise* or barbed wire were needed to keep him put. For that reason, the calaboose on Ocean Island was ill-fitted to contain inmates of a less home-staying habit. Our Chinese guests, for example, could and did escape from confinement practically whenever they liked and their midnight doings, together with those of their friends in the Chinese location, were a constant pain in the neck for the local administration. But although this did, as you will see, have a strong connection with my behaviour coming home from the manager's party, it wasn't the thing that actually drove me to drink while acting for Reggie McClure.

You might say that a microbe imported by Chinese labourers

was mainly to blame. I never saw a new draft of recruits from Hong Kong that failed to arrive in the pink of condition or omitted to bring with it an influenza germ of peculiar malignance. When the newcomers landed, the order of events never varied. Almost at once, the entire population of Gilbertese labourers would disappear into hospital. A week or so later, the British Phosphate Commissioners' staff of fifty odd Europeans would succumb *en masse* with their wives and families. The eleven hundred Ocean Islanders in their beautiful villages would follow. Last of all, when everyone else had forgotten what it felt like to be ill, came the turn of the wretched little government staff. And infallibly, at this point, the manager of the phosphate concern would decide to celebrate his complete return to health with a grand dinner-party.

So things fell out about three weeks before Reggie was due to return from leave. The manager's invitation came and was accepted at a moment when Olivia and I were the only representatives of His Majesty's local dignity still able to get up and stand on it. But by the date of the party Olivia was down with the usual fever and bone-ache (the thing was very like dengue); nobody else on the station was yet back on his feet; and I was obviously sickening for a nice little go of my own.

My temperature was over 100, and I shouldn't have thought twice about calling the fixture off under ordinary conditions. But I felt that Reggie, himself a model of official courtesy, might well be annoyed if he heard that not even the man acting for him had made an effort to attend.

Olivia told me from her bed of pain not to be an idiot, but I was set on going; so she said at last, oh well, if I had to be silly and official about it I had better fortify myself with a drop of the right stuff for a start and go on keeping up my strength with whatever I could lay my hands on as the evening proceeded.

A couple of whiskies before I left more than justified the

first part of her advice. Their effect on me was all the more bracing, I suppose, because at that age I hardly ever touched spirits. They sent me off humming gay little tunes along the lonely way to the manager's house. Another helpful thing they did (for that evening at least) was to break down the queasy dislike I had for dry Martinis and that grossly overrated beverage, champagne. Two or three of the former before dinner put me into fine shape for a methodical attack on the latter as soon as the excellent sherry they gave us had been faithfully dealt with. Some superb brandy when the ladies retired and I forget how many Scotches for the road at about 10.30 set me on my homeward path, if not in fact entirely cured of my temperature, at least too free from care to give a hoot whether I had one or not.

I remember still the chaste clarity, the shining happiness of my impressions as I floated home through the moonlight. I remember how the black and silver trees, and the great amethyst cloud galleons, and the darling honeysuckle stars between them, and the pale green sticks and stones that rolled beneath my feet seemed to murmur and ripple, and twinkle, and tinkle all together in an ecstasy of being that sang in perfect unison with my own as I climbed the craggy hillside. I remember shouting, "Here I come, laddie!" and dancing like a faun out on a gangplank over a forty-foot ravine that scared me silly when sober. I remember stopping on the other side to stand and gaze by a twisted rock, laughing for delight at the queer shadow it threw, and trying to strike the same attitude, and failing, and failing again, and laughing anew each time for the exquisite fun of being myself and not my flickering, futile shadow. The thing I really don't remember rightly is my motive for popping behind that rock when I saw the little Chinese figure creeping round a bend of the bush track ahead.

I knew, of course, that he could be up to no good. Though compound fences were forbidden, the Chinese and Gilbertese labourers were supposed to stay inside their respective bounds

M   169 after dark. But I must admit I wasn't troubling much about that kind of thing just then. I was simply brimming over with human affection, and I thought he was, too. Why, after all, probe deeper than that for motive?

"You funny ol', naughty ol', poor ol' boy!" I crooned towards him as he came sneaking nearer. "Caught in the act! But nemmind. Iss on'y good ol' Grumble!" And to convince him beyond all reasonable doubt of my pleasure at this meeting, I leapt out from behind the rock with whoopee after glad whoopee of friendship, and, arms flung high, rushed forward to embrace him there in that moonlit pathway.

I shall never forget the ungraciousness of his response. He stopped in his tracks; his hands flew up, clawing at his cheeks; his mouth fell open; he screamed one chattering, high-pitched scream when I was almost on top of him, then turned and hurled himself back along the way he had come.

The disappointment of it knocked all the sparkle out of me. I had no heart for chasing anyone who did not want my friendship. I sent a single wistful howl of farewell speeding in his wake and trudged the rest of the way home in melancholy silence.

The double doors of our bedroom were wide open to the verandah when I reached the residency, and I should easily have got to bed without disturbing my poor sick wife but for an architect's silly practical joke.

A batten of wood for the outside doors to close against in bad weather—a rain-stopper, I believe it was called—was nailed to the floor across the entrance. It had never been known to delay by an instant the flooding of the room in westerly squalls, but there it lurked, waiting for feet like mine to find it. Olivia woke with a shriek as all my bones hit the floor together.

I comforted her bravely from the dark where I grovelled "Issallri', my dear, issallri', iss on'y ol' Grumbo come 'ome."

Reassured, she sank into sleep again. But to me, as I lay gathering my forces, there came—I can't think why—a

170

sudden, overwhelming need to brush my hair. I rolled over on my back, groped upwards with one hand from where I lay, found the brush, jerked the runner off the dressing-table and brought its crockery crashing in ruin about my head.

Olivia woke with another shriek. There was a distinct touch of temper in it this time. "Are you by any chance tight?" she asked me, rather cruelly I thought.

Unwilling to return a sharp answer, I lay thinking it over soberly. "It mushta bin that terrible Chinese cocktail," I remember muttering just before sleep fell on me like an extinguisher, there on the cool, hard boards.

I woke up the next morning without a trace of fever and free of the smallest symptom of a hangover. The moral of this is that you can get a lot of good out of the creature if your limits are as moderate as mine were; and that is the proper climax of the story, but not the end of the record.

As soon as I was dressed, I went down to the police barracks for a talk with the Chinese interpreter and Sergeant-Major Taitusi. These illicit excursions of coolies from their locations must be stopped, I told them severely, after giving a rather modified rendering of my adventure.

There was a faint smile on the interpreter's face that I didn't much like. "Sir," he asked in his punctilious style, "is it possible that the evil fellow who escaped from your detaining hand last night was identical with the no-good convicted felon found missing from his prison cell at 10.44 and sought by us in vain until 10.58?"

"How should I know, man?" I replied irritably. "And while we're on it, why the deuce did you give up looking for him at 10.58?"

"Because at that time precisely, sir, he returned to us and desired with fearful pleadings to be locked up again."

I strongly hoped he would let it go at that, but he went on: "He deposed to the effect that an insane white man with the face of a devil pursued him through the bush with obvious intent to maim or murder."

"Why, the dirty liar!" I began indignantly, but his smooth voice continued as if I hadn't spoken, ". . . after due consideration, Sergeant-Major Taitusi and I are of the opinion that it was not a white man whom he saw, but one of the dangerous rock demons who are known to infest this island. There is a certain similarity . . ."

Did his wicked old eyelid flicker at me or not? I have never been sure. But I agreed with him heartily and suggested that, as the poor fellow had had such a fright we might with decency forbear to pursue the little matter of his temporary escape any further.

"That would indeed seem very just and proper," he answered urbanely. So the matter ended there.

10

Unofficial Interlude

The McClures returned to Ocean Island towards the middle
of 1925 from a four and a half months' tour of Japan and
Australia. In his brilliant, effortless way Reggie had written
the greater part of a book[1] at odd moments of his holiday
and also, while in Australia, had dashed off for the Sydney
Sunday Times a front-page article or two on Pacific naval
strategy. Writing, never less than an agony for my labouring
mind, was no more than an amusing relaxation for his swift
versatility. Nevertheless, the example of his successes did
decide me to try my luck at freelance journalism—though on
a less exalted plane than his—when next I went on leave to
Sydney.

As things fell out, that 'next' had to be almost at once.
Less than a year back on the equator had already drained poor
Olivia's cheeks of all their English pink and reduced her once
more to the frail ghost she had been in 1920, after our first

[1] Later published under the title *Land Travel and Seafaring*

six years in the islands. I too was more like a wraith than a human being, for I hadn't yet managed to shake off all the effects of that sorcerer's dose of cantharides. For these reasons, our eighteen weeks of leave together in Australia were spent convalescing in perfect idleness at Turramurra (in those days one of Sydney's still rustic North Shore suburbs) and never a notion of breaking into journalism recurred to me until Olivia had to leave again for England.

But then the doctor suddenly said I needed another six weeks of his treatment, which brought me hard up against the question of finance. By that time all the full-pay leave due to me had run out: a six weeks' extension could therefore only be granted on half pay, and half pay was not even enough to maintain the family in England, let alone a father idling in Australia. It was in this dilemma that I turned to journalism for help. Wasting no time in struggling to emulate Reggie's superb front-page achievement, I began to grind out anonymous news paragraphs of the hit or miss kind for several Sydney dailies and single-column signed articles for those which ran weekly magazine pages.

Every Saturday morning (if I remember the day aright) I would queue up at their various pay desks with other contributors of my sort and, after producing evidence of identity and publication, rake in the fees with which—at two guineas a column for stories or articles and rates ranging between an honest penny and a princely twopence a line for paragraphs—they were good enough to reward our industry. It was contrary to colonial regulations and sadly discordant with every accepted notion of proconsular dignity, but the fun of it was more stimulating than all the physic in the world. It added 8 pounds to my weight in a fortnight. More important still, it increased my income by altogether £24 12s. 4d., and this easily covered my personal maintenance including doctor's bills, while a small advance against salary from our very kind Colony Agents, Burns, Philp & Company, closed every other gap on the domestic front until I got back to full pay again.

But this happy interlude of rebellion had lasted only four weeks when poor Reggie was found by the doctor at Ocean Island to have a heart murmur and had to be sent by the next ship to Sydney for further diagnosis. Luckily there was a sailing from Sydney to Ocean Island the day after he left, which landed me back on the equator, with orders to act for him once more, almost as soon as he reached Australia.

The Methvens being still away at Fanning Island, no huge and smiling Stuartson was in the boat that came out to take me ashore. But a new friend—Jack Blaikie, ex-airman of the Great War, whom the education department of Victoria had lately lent us as headmaster of our government school for Baanaban boys—was at the boat harbour to give me a welcome. I couldn't stay at the residency, he told me, as Mrs. McClure had not left with Reggie; so would I care to put up with him and his wife until further notice? I jumped at the offer, and thus it came about in the fullness of time—meaning about a month from then—that poor Dorothy Blaikie's bungalow on the crest of the slope that fell away south-eastwards to the B.P.C.'s settlement at Uma was turned into a kind of guardroom and general rendezvous for everyone who had anything to do with the handling of the Chinese riot.

Dies Irae

The riot happened on a day somewhere near the middle of October. The Chinese opened the show with a raid on the Gilbertese labour location, to which they had dedicated months of preparation. Though the weapons of the rank and file were simple bars of iron, the most loving thought had been spent on arms for their leaders. The Generalissimo and his three Generals carried ancient revolvers smuggled in from Hong Kong; Colonels and Majors dispensed jam-jar and salmon-tin bombs of local manufacture; Captains and Lieutenants had the privilege of wielding the most romantic-looking

175

scimitars from behind corrugated-iron shields and bucklers of curious design.

Gelignite for the bombs had been stolen fragment by fragment, detonators one by one, fuse a few inches at a time, from the white overseers responsible for blasting operations. It twists the heart queerly in retrospect to think of the piled-up patiences that went to the making of those bombs, and of the pains so tenderly lavished upon the fashioning of the little scimitars; for the bombs were hardly more lethal than rather big crackers and the scimitars, so bright, so beautifully curved, were piteously ineffective against the rude Gilbertese bludgeons and rocks; and I don't believe that either was really meant to kill. What I do believe is that both they and the aged revolvers of the Generals were, like the grandiose military titles themselves, just the wistful bang-crash-flashing *panache* or artists starved of romance—symbols of a desperately felt right to glory brandished in the teeth of a cold alien world.

The plan of battle, already hatched and written down months before the day of the riot, was to catch the hated Gilbertese workers at their most vulnerable moment; that is, while enjoying their lunch in the big open-sided messroom fifty yards uphill from the northern boundary of the Chinese location. It was laid down in the orders that three columns, each about 200 strong (and each led by a General firing his revolver, a Colonel and two Majors tossing their bombs, four Captains and eight Lieutenants striking their scimitars with frightful clashing noises upon their corrugated shields), should emerge from different parts of their location and, rushing upon the messroom from its eastern, southern and western sides respectively, drive the terrified enemy with intimidating shouts and painful blows of their iron bars northwards up the hillside, into the ignominious shelter of their own sleeping quarters.

If there was any offensive intent beyond this climax neither the written plan nor the evidence taken after the event had anything to say about it. The testimony offered to me months

later by the Generalissimo, just before his release from prison,
was that the men with the iron bars had been definitely in-
structed to give up intimidating the Gilbertese as soon as these
had dived into their funk-holes. After that point, it seemed,
the magnanimous host was to have marched from the field in
disdainful silence, leaving the stricken islanders alone with
their humiliation.

All warlike stores and equipment having been assembled
by early October, nothing remained then for the dedicated six
hundred but to await the next reasonable cause of battle.
The precipitating event occurred towards the middle of the
month, when a Gilbertese youth jerked a ladder from under a
Chinese house-painter and his paint-pot. It was a loutish
trick, enough to have caused a general sit-down strike at any
time. But nobody flung his tools down that day. A war
council was held instead, that same evening, in the Chinese
location; and next day, according to plan, the triple assault
upon the Gilbertese messroom was launched.

Jack Blaikie and I were sitting on his verandah ready for
lunch when the sound of an explosion, and then another, came
up to us from the Uma settlement. Had there been no more
than a couple of bangs like that, we wouldn't have noticed
them—blasting was always going on somewhere on the island
—but these bangs were followed hard by three or four pops
like pistol-shots and a clamour of distant shouting. We jumped
from our seats, staring at each other. "I bet that's the Chinese!"
exclaimed Blaikie, inspired I don't know how, and next
moment both of us were out of the house plunging down the
path to Uma as fast as our legs would take us. We hardly
noticed the sudden rain that lashed us as we ran.

We came panting to the narrow-gauge railway line that
divided the two locations. By that time the attack, so
laboriously prepared, so proudly launched, was already
smashed to bits. The Gilbertese issuing lunchless and furious
from their messrooms (a few of them smarting damnably
from nails and scrap-iron implanted in their anatomies by the

two bombs we had heard) had counter-attacked on the spot with rocks torn from the borders of their location footpath. A good half of the Chinese had incontinently fled back to the shelter of their sleeping quarters. The rest, split into a dozen fragments, were still hanging about just out of range of the Gilbertese rocks, while half a dozen of the B.P.C.'s white staff and five or six Ellice Island policemen, all unarmed, rushed back and forth trying to get everyone to go home.

Blaikie raced ahead of me a hundred yards to the major centre of trouble east of the messroom; I stayed on the hither side, by a wooden bridge on the roadway above the railway line, where Sergeant Nape stood opposing his mighty chest and fourteen stone of Ellice Island brawn to twenty-one scimitars and a pistol whose owners were screaming to get by him, back into the fray. Fifty yards down the road, armed with bludgeons, shovels and rocks, waited a score of Gilbertese, roaring at him to let the little men pass.

What knocked at my heart as I scrambled up the bank to join Nape was that, for all their fury of impatience to get him out of the way, not one of those men raised a weapon against him, while he, on his side, never once drew his truncheon to drive them back. When they did at last manage to shift him aside, it was by dint of forming a crocodile scrum of fours behind fours and heaving against him with the united thrust of forty-four legs. Just as I reached the level of the pathway, he popped out of the bridge-end like a cork from a ginger beer bottle and rolled on his back:

"Sillipuggers, sillipuggers!" he bawled at me as the forty-four legs rushed over him. "They gerremselves dead longa Gilibert boys too quick!" and, leaping up, flung himself in headlong chase—the perfect gentle policeman that he was—to save them if he could from the results of their own foolishness. I found myself dashing beside him through the puddles close on the heels of the rearmost warrior, who happened to be a wild-haired, pistol-brandishing General.

That flourished gun most kindly ceased at once to cause me any anxiety because, under my eyes as he ran, the General suddenly pulled it down from the air and, with a series of the most artistically blood-curdling yells, emptied its six chambers into the earth. This seemed to me proof enough of its strictly aesthetic intentions on the field of battle. Nape, however, decided on his own account against leaving it with him, and, taking a diagonal dive at his back, brought him down in the slush immediately under my feet. The gun flew forward from his outflung hand and I like an arrow after it in a belly-dive over their bodies. I didn't care what happened to it after that. Nape and I sat there recovering ourselves while the scimitar men, unhindered, rushed upon their fate. "Silli-puggers! Sillipuggers!" roared Nape again as we watched them piteously break and melt away for the second time that day before the Gilbertese counter-attack, leaving four men wounded on the pathway. We managed to get some dejected stragglers to pick these up—they weren't very badly hurt—and bear them uphill to the hospital. The General had dis-appeared.

I personally saw no more of the fighting than that small sideshow. But things had been more serious at Blaikie's end. A savage Gilbertese sortie had cut off the retreat of some iron-bar men into their own location and left one of them pulped to death, with seven others only just alive strewn around him, on the slope above the boat harbour. There had been ferocious clashes, too, on the higher levels. Yet, by the time Nape and I got there, Blaikie and his half-dozen fellow Australians with a few unarmed policemen had already contrived to shepherd most of the Chinese back into their location. That was a job which many times their number of armed men could never have managed without inviting more bloodshed; and the special constables who, for the next week or so, stood on guard un-armed between the two locations made the only kind of 'force' that could peaceably have prevented the Gilbertese—seething still to show how deeply they scorned firearms of any kind—from launching a night raid, with all-out slaughter, on their wretched enemies.

And so those proud attackers finished (in the words of our Chinese interpreter) as "the humbled objects of our solicitous moral defence." That was a sad come-down for them at the time. Nevertheless, by my reckoning, it cost them no loss of face in the end, because the riot they had staged made it impossible for anyone to ignore their genuine grievances any longer. The British Phosphate Commissioners found themselves obliged at last to invest a bit of money and thought in their security. A beautiful new Chinese location was built up the hillside, a mile away from the Gilbertese quarters, and the two labour forces were set to work in mining areas and workshops well apart from each other.

Alas, however, the first thing to be done when things simmered down a little was to bring a few responsible people to account. Not that anybody regretted the imprisonment of the Gilbertese youth who had upset the painter and his pot. But it was more difficult to spot the villains on the Chinese side. The iron-bar men could hardly be regarded as ringleaders and the rôle of the scimitar men had clearly been little more than that of artists in a state of effervescence. The same was of course true of the top-rankers, too, with their big titles and little bombs and aged revolvers; but the law never can altogether condone the use of guns and explosives in an affray, so it was these who had to suffer. Also, because death had come to one and wounds to many, the sentences had to be more than a joke. The Generalissimo and his three Generals got a year's hard labour each.

Cryptic New Friend

When the General whom Nape had bowled over was brought in for trial, his first act was to step up to the court table and lay his gun before me. "It is unloaded," explained the gentlemanly Ellice Island constable in charge, "and he very much wanted to hand it over himself, so we let him."

"But wasn't this taken from you that day at Uma?" I asked the General, a grim-looking character much more heavily boned and muscled than the average of his fellows.

No, the interpreter told me after some talk with him: the fact was that when he and Nape and I had crashed together in the pathway he had been the first to get up (because Nape had struck his head on a rock and I was ignominiously winded, my mind corroborated him). Picking up his gun before either of us was in a state to notice much, he had slipped quietly off to the Chinese location, where the weapon had lain hidden ever since.

"But what about the search?" I spoke rather indignantly because, ten days after the riot, a landing party from H.M. sloop *Veronica* had helped us to comb the location for concealed arms and explosives as a preliminary to allowing the Chinese back to work again.

The interpreter smiled apologetically. "Ah . . . the search," he murmured ". . . it is to be assumed, I fear, that the prisoner did not altogether approve of that operation."

"Didn't approve . . . ?" I repeated blankly.

There was a little more talk between the two. Then the interpreter explained, "Only the local government, in his humble opinion, is entitled to receive the surrender of his weapon."

From the impersonal stare of the prisoner I couldn't guess whether this was meant as a high courtesy or a crushing reproach; but I distinctly felt he had won the first round, either way; something queerly like an aura of authority emanated from him as he stood there barefoot in his tattered canvas shorts and stained sweat-rag.

As an indictable offence was at issue, our court was sitting with two assessors on the bench. One of these now pointed out that the prisoner had not as yet been fairly put on his defence and so ought to be told at once that nothing he had so far done or said before us could be used in evidence against him.

The General listened with a strained frown while the interpreter explained this point and also the further nicety that I, as his judge, was debarred from testifying to anything I may have seen him do during the riot. I have never seen bewilderment written plainer on any face than on his as he stood in silence before replying; and I shall never forget the half tolerant, half contemptuous smile he gave me, or the odd gesture he made—as if to push aside invisible cobwebs from his eyes—as he answered, "There is my gun. You know what I did. I was a leader," and left it at that.

"Well, advise him at least to plead Not Guilty to the charge," I told the interpreter forlornly: "Sergeant Nape's the only witness for the prosecution, and he might not be able to swear to the man's identity."

"I am guilty," was his only answer to this, while the gaze he fixed on me said as plainly as if he had shouted the words, "To hell with all this hoky-poky and let's get straight to the facts." And again I felt that strange emanation of authority from him.

The only form of 'hard labour' at our headquarters gaol that qualified for so stern a name was that of humping sand and shingle from a beach near Tabiang village to the public works yard on top of the island. Every medically fit prisoner had to put in two days a week at this chore, and everyone (barring that tragic lapse of Teakai's) had always been allowed to go very easy on it. But the General wanted no such indulgence. He set so monstrous an example of industry filling bags and rushing them up the steep hillside that, before his first month was out, his all-Chinese working party was begging to be rid of his company. The warders heartily backed the petition. They too were tired to death of trying to keep him in sight uphill.

We set him next to sawing logs for firewood. (Free fuel for the kitchen stove was every local official's celestial privilege

182

in those spacious days, and great was the demand for it every morning). But the trouble here for the General was that it takes two—one at each end—to keep a crosscut saw going. It was our trouble too. We couldn't very well reproach him for putting his whole strength into the work, neither could we decently penalize his successive mates for refusing to work at his fearful speed.

If only he had taken things a bit more cheerfully all round, he might not have got himself so hated. But he just hurled himself at every task, his grim jaw set, his eyes unsmiling and aloof, as if not a warder or a fellow prisoner existed for him except to be shown up as a slacker. Feeling got so hot about him in the end that the only thing to do was to invent a special job for him absolutely apart from everyone else. I don't know who first thought of turning him loose on the so-called vegetable garden at the residency, but I found him waiting for me there with the interpreter one morning when I went up to work in Reggie's private office.

We trooped together round the desolate half-acre of flat ground between the back yard and the servants' quarters. Once upon a time, somebody had tried to start a kitchen garden there, but the hopeless battle with the sterile soil—almost pure phosphate of lime, insoluble in water—had long been abandoned. Not even the weeds grew freely in that sun-smitten square of dust and crumbling rocks.

But the General's gaze was fixed on the deep forest of calophyllum trees that marched right up to the edge of our clearing. Could he go in there and cut what sticks he liked and dig as much leaf mould as he wanted, he asked. And could he have a spade, and a fork, and a mattock, and a hoe, and an axe, and a saw? And could we spare a wheelbarrow, not forgetting some planks to wheel it on from the forest to the garden? And would we let him build a little leaf shack there for all his tools? And might he sit in it to eat at midday instead of wasting time going down to the prison cook-house? And might he get back to work again as soon as ever he liked after eating? And would we this, and might he that or the other thing, and so on, and so on—he stood there forgetful of his prison clothes pelting us with endless questions, a man with suddenly shining eyes lost in a vision of himself creating a garden in a wilderness. I never saw him without a smile on his face from that day forward.

The residency orderly was supposed to take charge of him at eight every morning, and so he did in a strictly official sense for the first week or so. After that, however, it wasn't a prisoner but a master craftsman that he went to watch. He would sit fascinated for hours together on the kitchen steps while, stroke by stroke of mattock, spade and hoe, barrow by barrow of leaf mould from the forest, the General laid down the first few perches of his garden, And then, before a month was out, the orderly was down to the job himself, making mat shelters and seedling boxes for a nursery under the General's direction. And the week after that, the residency cook had joined him as a learner. I watched them both taking instructions on how to set up a cover of loose leaves on six-foot stilts over the whole new plot before the General—plainly now the officer in charge of everything—went off to dig more trenches, and cut more stakes, and cart more earth for more and more plots beyond it.

And so he continued, his daily output that of any three average navvies, until he had laid out two more plots as big as the first and was half-way towards finishing yet another. But then the plants in his original plot began to flower, and all at once he was a different man. He dug no more trenches, left the new beds to lie fallow and worked happily all day among the green things he had brought to life. It was as if the promise of their fruition had stilled at last some savage unrest in his heart and called a truce to his wild industry.

Or perhaps he felt that what they needed now to bring them into fullest bearing was an infusion of his own strong spirit. The way he talked to them as he watered their roots or simply stood silent, empty can in hand, brooding over them, suggested some kind of spiritual outpouring. Or so, at least the interpreter thought, and I found his theory easy to believe when I came to taste of the fruits of the garden. The General's tomatoes and pumpkins, melons and runner beans were certainly the best I had ever eaten in the tropics.

He and his fellow Generals had served no more than eight months of their sentence when a chance came to return them to Hong Kong, and we decided not to miss it. (I was Resident Commissioner myself by that time.) They were released three days before their ship sailed so as to give them plenty of time to pack up and say good-bye to their friends. They left the prison at 6 a.m. but the General, dressed now in a neat jumper suit of dark blue denim and shouldering a small wooden chest, was back at the residency with the interpreter before midday. He asked for permission to sleep in his tool-shed for the next three nights, because that would enable him to spend a little more time with his plants and his friends.

The friends he meant were, of course, the orderly and the cook, from whom he had picked up an astonishingly fluent gabble of Gilbertese. Both were delighted at his return and the cook, a family man, insisted on taking him into his own house. That was the first and last time I ever saw an islander grant this particular honour to anyone but a relation by blood or marriage. It was an enormous success. When I looked in on the family after dinner, there was the General sitting on the guest mat with the latest baby in his arms and two little girls cuddling up to him on either side.

The day his ship sailed, he brought the interpreter to my office for an early morning farewell. He plunged without preliminaries, rather to my surprise, into a statement of his immediate plans. He had a mother, a wife and two children, he said, who lived on a piece of land that he owned outside the city of Canton. He had left them several years ago to seek his fortune alone in foreign parts. But now he was going back to them, because here, on Ocean Island, he had come to understand that they were his real fortune.

"The clear implication is," explained the interpreter—"that this revelation had come to him through the garden you have so courteously allowed him to make and the family life into which the cook has so graciously admitted him."

"I'm delighted to hear it," I said, more than a little touched, "and I'm sure the cook would be, too."

"He has already returned thanks to the cook," replied the interpreter, "and all that remains for him to do now is to thank you too in the same manner. Being far from his native land, he is, to his sorrow, unable to bring with him the kind of gift that he would have wished to lay before you on such an occasion as this, but he begs you to accept instead the enclosed quite unworthy, nevertheless entirely sincere, token of his gratitude and respect." Having said which, he laid on the desk before me an O.H.M.S. envelope, obviously borrowed from my office, containing a £1 note.

"But you know I can't take this from him," I exclaimed when I had recovered from the shock of it.

"To avoid serious loss of face on the giver's part," he replied imperturbably, "I advise acceptance with immediate and profuse expressions of appreciation. A return gift of, say, five times the value somewhat later in the day should suffice to maintain your own prestige in the matter."

So I accepted the General's gift and received for further recompense a handclasp as warm and friendly as any a brother man ever honoured me with. Some hours later he left the residency all smiles with two precious tinned hams and a sackful of other provisions from my store cupboard slung over his shoulder, while the orderly followed carrying his little box, and the cook's two children trotted alongside, weeping profusely, to see him off.

But a week or so after he was gone it was still on my mind that I had repaid him in kind instead of money. "He couldn't have saved much out of his wages," I said to the interpreter one day: "nearly half his time here was spent in prison, poor fellow."

"It is a fact," he replied, "that the money he had could hardly be called savings. Nevertheless, 'poor fellow' is an epithet I should hesitate to apply to him. He left the island with some eight hundred £1 notes in his chest."

"Eight hundred? Impossible. Why, his pay . . ." I began, but he cut me short: "Not pay but winnings. Winnings at mah-jong and fan-tan. That was why he was so eager to go to prison. Nobody could win it back from him up here."

"A truly complicated character," he added as he turned to leave me, and I let it rest at that.

Formula for a Fence

The great majority of the Chinese on Ocean Island were good citizens. Nevertheless, there were always lawless elements among them, and most of our headaches in that lovely little place came from the fact that we were not allowed to control the doings of the midnight-minded by enclosing their settlement in a nice tall steel fence.

The official situation was a very tricky one. Although over a quarter of a century had passed since the Chinese labour scandals in South Africa had overthrown a government in England, the words 'compound,' 'enclosure' and even 'fence' were still politically anathema in Whitehall, and the Colonial Office was frightened into fits by any proposal to surround anyone at all with anything more substantial than a cobweb.

It was stupid indeed of me to forget about all that in 1927, when I put up my ingenuous scheme for establishing all-round safety on Ocean Island. But I was still handicapped by the belief that what Secretaries of State wanted most from the grand old colonial service was the truth about the actual needs of colonial populations. Under this pious illusion, I reported how bold by night a lawless element among the Chinese labourers was becoming, how alarmingly for everyone the crimes of burglary and housebreaking had increased, how impossible for a police force short of an army it was, without an enclosing fence and floodlights, to prevent marauders from issuing at will from the Chinese reserve to prowl through the British Phosphate Commissioners' unprotected settlements.

The answer from Whitehall was a cold despatch to the High Commissioner, who had backed my proposals, pointing out that any such enclosure of indentured Chinese within a fence as I had proposed was out of the question.

Reading back into the files then, and balancing one thing with another, I got my first real inkling of how much more in those days the Colonial Office had to worry about the political safety of the Secretary of State than about the physical safety of any colonial population. This lesson having been digested, and the plague of housebreaking remaining constant, the obvious thing to do was to offer the Secretary of State a much more attractive political reason for granting what we needed than the mere proof of how urgent our need was.

A dear little Gilbertese boy of five or six stepped in to help us at this point. He walked one afternoon on the edge of the Chinese location, innocently throwing stones at birds, and one of his shots fell near a coolie who stood watching him. Though the man was not actually hit, he had to skip aside very suddenly to save his shins, and there was immediate uproar. The child was not harmed, but held and brought yelling to the residency by a deputation of twenty men. The idea was that his father had maliciously delegated him to do their colleague grievous bodily harm, and must be made to pay instant compensation.

I had to tell them that, since nobody had in fact been hurt, it wasn't likely that he would agree to pay anything. But I had learned by then that you must never send a Chinese deputation away absolutely empty; the maintenance of face demanded that they should leave with something positive to tell their fellow countrymen. So, casting around rather hopelessly for the right thing to say, I asked them at random if they and their friends wouldn't like to have a beautiful, unscalable, expanded steel fence put up around their location to protect them from prowling stone-throwers—a fence with gloriously bright arc-lamps set along it at intervals to tell their protectors, our police, of the approach of enemies out of the darkness; a fence . . . well, I admit I became inspired at that point. I suddenly had a vision of the Secretary of State for the Colonies goggling at me as I added detail after shocking detail to the enclosing fence of my dreams. From then on, I fear, the wistful fun of it engaged me more than the actual business of the deputation.

I was the more astounded, therefore, at the clamour of agreement that greeted my forlorn flight of fancy. Nothing, they said, could possibly be more to their liking than the notion of being enclosed day and night with a 10-foot fence such as I had described, provided only one thing, which was that it must be topped off with the crowning glory of another three feet of wire bristling with barbs. The knowledge of being thus securely protected from their alleged protectors, the police, as well as from all their other enemies, they said, would at last give all of them a sense of being permanently safe in, and masters of, their very own piece of territory. They indicated that the good work had better be put in hand pretty soon, or else . . .

I promised with sudden new hope to use all my personal pull with the King of England himself to persuade him to order their employer to give them their heart's desire.

The child and his father forgotten, they hurried off to spread the grand news far and wide. The same evening, I drafted a despatch carefully devoid of reference to any previous correspondence on the subject of fences. The capture, after a struggle, of the stone-thrower (a male; age omitted) by the gravely alarmed Chinese and the subsequent deputation clamouring at the gates of the residency for some sort of permanent protection made nice copy, even in officialese. So did the closing recommendations, if I may say so. Everything, of course, depended at that point upon avoiding any mention of the forbidden words. The proposed fence accordingly became 'a series of excluding barriers of expanded steel,' and these barriers, instead of being built to surround or enclose anyone in the world, had to be 'erected in the neighbourhood of the Chinese location in such a manner as to afford the inhabitants maximum protection on every hand against unfriendly intrusions from outside.' I draw particular attention to the words 'maximum protection,' meaning roughly an unbroken ring of steel.

We were allowed to proceed almost at once with our Great Wall of Chinatown. (Officialese has its uses, after all.)

A Cure for Toothache

Medically speaking, the only real discomfort of Ocean Island was the want of a dentist. If clove oil did your toothache no good, you either sat tight and stuck out the attack up there on the equator or make tracks for your favourite practitioner in Sydney, 2,400 miles away.

In 1930, when my left lower what-not began to give me gyp, I was only just back from long leave in England and hadn't a hope of getting it attended to in Australia until 1932 at earliest. Of course, kind Dr. Gould at the hospital would have whipped it out for me, if I had asked him to, but I didn't want to lose it; on the other hand, it was playing the devil with my work; I don't know what I should have done about it had not Providence most kindly and efficiently settled the matter for me out of hand.

The curative process began at about 5.15 on a fine Saturday afternoon when I was nursing and cursing a particularly scarlet dose of pain. There came a sudden telephone call from Alec Goudy, the Manager of the fine, new, recently fenced-in Chinese labourer's location. "Can you hear me?" came his cautious whisper over the line. "Well, they've got me locked in here; but they've forgotten I can use the phone."

'Here,' it turned out, was Alec's small office inside the location, while 'they' were a dozen or so Chinese who had hustled him into it and were now standing on guard outside the door. Their grudge against him was that he had tried to rescue an unfortunate man whom some others had tied to a post and were in the act of flogging. The Chinese 'people's court,' they told him, had convicted this man of being a police spy (which, by the way, he wasn't) and had sentenced him to receive a thousand strokes of the cane. The labourers intended to dedicate their Saturday evening not to mah-jong or other games as usual, but to executing the judgment of the court. "They're still beating the poor devil," Alec's final whisper told me. "I can hear the welts from here. Come quickly. You'll find him tied to one of the big posts in the east side of the recreation hall."

The Chinese 'people's court' was a new one on me, and it looked bad. Nevertheless, hurrying down to the barracks, I had to think carefully about using the police as a rescue squad. Standing instructions said I mustn't resort to force until I had made sure that nothing short of it would save the wretched man's bacon. The only way to get that point established was to go alone into the location for a start.

However, I did feel entitled to take a few simple precautions. So we arranged that, five minutes after I had started for the location, Sergeant-Major Taitusi should take up his stand outside a small gate at its western end. If I failed to appear there within fifteen minutes of his arrival, he was to conclude that I hadn't proved a success as a peacemaker. Whereupon, he would lead in a detachment of twenty men armed with truncheons, make for the recreation hall, find out what was happening there, and do whatever had to be done to get the beaten man (and, incidentally, me too) out of trouble.

It struck me to hope very sincerely, on my quarter-mile walk to the location, that the element of adventure in the errand I had let myself in for would one day afford me much more pleasure in retrospect than I was extracting from the immediate prospect of it. With toothache, it is hard to imagine oneself a devil of a fellow or comport oneself with the authentic Big White Master swagger.

Not a sound of strife reached me as I entered the location. The quiet of the evening hour lay upon the neat little two-roomed sleeping houses strung in terraced rows above and below the path I followed. Someone on a verandah was singing a small falsetto song to the dying day. The touching, childlike voice rose, fell, fluttered, as aimless and happy as a butterfly in the golden light: there was remote peace in the eyes that watched me pass. I had a sense of leaving them a thousand miles away as I rounded the shoulder of the hillside and came in sight of the recreation hall.

The hall was a single long room stepped up the hillside on a series of terraced floors, so that these formed a stage above the bottom end. As its sides were completely open, you could enter where you liked by ducking in under the low-hung eaves. But that day a swarm of labourers blocked the way in on to the lower floors, intent on what was happening down left of them, and I had to slip in at the top end. As I came up at it from behind their right shoulders, not a soul noticed me. I was three-quarters of the way down the central flight of steps inside before anyone knew I was there.

What took me down at a run was the sickening swish and swat of a half-inch cane on a human body. They had their man tied to a stud on the left side of the hall, at the level, so to speak, of the orchestra stalls. He had been made fast with his face to the post. His head lolled sideways on his shoulder; I thought his neck was broken; it seemed impossible that he could take those terrible swinging welts without a move unless every spark of life had left him. I forgot my toothache for the moment.

I found myself standing by the man, ringed round by a gaping wordless mob. But I was not alone. There beside me, his young face wreathed in smiles, stood Takinaiti.

Takinaiti was a Gilbertese boy of seventeen, fresh from our small government training school at Tarawa, now learning his job as clerk-interpreter at headquarters office. He knew perfectly well that his race made him the natural target for the anger of every man in that hall. There was bitter hate between Chinese and Gilbertese in those days. But there he was, as welcome as an angel, in his beautiful white waistcloth hemmed with scarlet braid.

"You young fool!" I hissed at him. "What are you doing here?"

His smile never wavered. "I thought you might need me," he explained. "Can I do anything to help?"

"Certainly you can," I was only too glad to tell him. "Run quick and tell Sergeant-Major Taitusi to bring those men along straight away."

He turned and pushed his way calmly through the crowd. They actually made way for him. He gave me a wave as he left the hall. I suddenly felt fine.

All that had taken only seconds. I turned at once to the bound man, but I had done no more than pluck futilely at the iron-hard knots that held him when everyone started to jabber and scream, and a dozen hands snatched me away from his side.

Nobody tried to hurt me. All they did was to swing me round to face the crowd, then drop my arms. But it was clear enough that they weren't going to let the man go without some kind of fuss. The only sensible thing to do from then on, was to play for time. Rather less than five minutes should see the police there, I reckoned, as I shouted into the clamour, "Can anybody here speak English?"

A tiny gamecock of a man strutted forward. "I do," he said, and explained in faultless English that the man tied to the stud had been sentenced by a properly constituted 'people's court,' whose judgment I would interfere with at my peril. He turned then and addressed the crowd, verbosely telling them, I supposed, how rudely he was dealing with me. All that accounted for something over two minutes. The succeeding clamour of applause for him and derision for me took up another thirty seconds at least. I imagined the police just on their way, at the double, when my turn came to speak again.

I began with the sort of line bureaucrats are bound to shoot about the sovereignty of British courts in British territory and all that. Then there had to be something about the naughtiness of locking Alec Goudy in his office. What with this, plus the frills he added in translation, plus the renewed screaming that followed, another good three minutes had trickled by when he turned and gibed, "You have less than forty police altogether and we Chinese are more than seven hundred strong; so what are you going to do about it?"

And still no police appeared.

But I knew it could only be a matter of seconds now. The thing most likely to hold their attention as long as that was to read them the riot act. It was a fair thing to warn them, anyway. So I told them what Takinaiti had gone to do, and advised them to get out of the hall if they wanted to avoid the police truncheons. But before I was through, a small two-seater bench came sailing through the air from somewhere on my left and knocked me spinning.

"This is the end," I thought as I went down. And in that very moment the police arrived.

As I picked myself up, not a soul was looking at me. There was hardly a soul left in the hall to do so. Practically the whole boiling—maybe four hundred or so of them—had rushed out with axes, pickaxes, crowbars and shovels to swarm around the file of big brown men who, two by two in perfect order, came swinging down the hillside.

All my life I have been an enemy of force, but I still remember with delight the way that small detachment used its twenty truncheons. Our police were carefully taught to respect Chinese skulls and spleens, and respect them these men did with perfection of restraint the whole way down. I am not saying they didn't land some shrewd knocks on shoulders and knee-joints. Outnumbered by twenty to one as they were, and up against weapons which, for all their crudeness, were lethal, they had to do that or stand and be brained. But it was the least, not the most use they could make of their arms, and I felt like crying for pride of their gentleness as, bleeding from many a wound, they ploughed their patient furrow through the attack of that yelling mob.

They ringed us round and held up every charge while one of them helped me to get the victim untied. Then, head first and face up a constable for each arm and leg, his poor sagging wisp of a body was carried out, with three files of two men each clearing the way before him, five pairs following after to cope with attacks from flanks and rear, and myself at the tail-end of the crocodile, once again nursing and cursing a tooth which seven new devils had suddenly reoccupied.

The first objective of our little crawling procession was the path by which I had come in, between the terraced sleeping houses. Only fifty yards of open country divided us from it, but here, where our right flank was exposed to attack from uphill, was where the enemy now gathered all his forces for a counterstroke. While the main group stood showering us with brickbats from above, a spearhead suddenly burst from among them with the master weapon—an extra long wooden bench from the recreation hall. Wielding it in the manner of a battering ram, a suicide squad of eighteen chosen stalwarts— nine a side—came charging down upon us, hell for leather, yelling at the top of their lungs, straight for the body of their senseless compatriot.

They fortunately missed a direct hit, because the man's bearers, with extraordinary coolness, leapt backwards with him in the last tick of time. But he did not entirely escape damage. The bench caught him a glancing blow on the head and by some extraordinary chance, lifted the scalp whole from his skull, so that it hung by no more than a hinge of flesh from his forehead.

The suicide squad, clinging to their now unmanageable monster, were whirled by its momentum clean through the gaping rank, which promptly closed after their passage, while they, their intemperately twinkling little legs no longer able to cope, suddenly collapsed in a deplorable bunch and went madly bounding, heels over head, one over another, down the rugged hillside.

They must have hurt themselves a lot. The sight wrung a

fulfilled laugh even out of my toothache, and, ten seconds later, Providence sent me a still more precious reward. We were just winning to the cover of the sleeping-houses, and I had turned back to hurry up a pair of constables who had straggled, when the miraculous stone arrived.

It must have been a stone of extraordinary shape. I always pictured it to myself rather like a bird's head with a delicate, longish, curved beak. Delicate or not, this beaked thing came flying down from some inspired Chinese hand, pecked a neat hole through my lower lip, bit into the gum, excised my aching tooth—none other—without the least damage to either of its neighbours, and, as Heaven is my witness, whipped it, absolutely entire, half-way out into daylight through the little pecked hole; so that when, having clapped a hand to my mouth, I drew it away to stare at the blood on it, there was that miserable bit of ivory stuck between my fingers.

I would have paused then to look for that amazing and beneficent stone but for one circumstance. The other end of it, perhaps more crudely shaped than the beak, had made such a horrid mess of my upper lip and four perfectly good teeth in the top jaw that I was left, for the moment, devoid of any intelligent curiosity about anything.

Looking back, the only fault I can find with the behaviour of Providence that day, was the price it charged the police for the relief of my toothache. Every man of them was badly cut about; it was a month before many of them were on their feet again. The man whose life they had saved came off much cheaper. The doctor simply washed his head, fitted the scalp back on it in the manner of a skullcap, sewed the edges round, kept him in bed, and there he was within a fortnight looking as if he had never had to turn a hair.

He asked to see me when he came out of hospital. I was glad to agree; I knew the police would appreciate a word of thanks from him. But gratitude wasn't exactly what he had in mind. His line was that the police had assumed entire responsibility for his safety by removing him, without his consent, from the recreation hall. That being so, they should have been quicker on their feet when the charge with the bench happened. Their slowness had cost him a month's idleness in hospital. What he wanted to know was how much compensation the government proposed to pay him. The intrepreter said there were no words in his language to render my reply.

Swan Songs

There were some things that the white man—the Man of Matang—might, with benefit, have left behind him when he came in strength to the Pacific; there were others that, had he brought them in greater measure, would have softened the impact and might have provided a stronger bond between the hearts of the strangers and the islanders. Song, it seems to me, was one of these.

I had been speaking to a clever old native of the Gilbert Islands about aeroplanes and wireless. When I had done, he pondered a little, then said, "Kurimbo, it is true the white man can fly; he can speak across the ocean; in works of the body he is indeed greater than we, but"—his voice rang with pride—"he has no songs like ours, no poets to equal the island singers."

In his ignorance, this old brown warrior thought of us as an utterly material race, destitute of the gift of poetry. We smile with half-pitying tolerance at such unenlightenment—yet how do we think of the islander? Many of us picture him as a savage, pleasant-mannered enough to visit in an idle hour, rather an attractive person altogether and good local colour, but still a savage, having nothing of wisdom or grace in his culture that could possibly command a white man's reverence. As a poet whose work might bear comparison with that of our own master singers, we simply do not think of him. My years among the natives of the Gilbert Islands taught me how mistaken we are.

The islander is a consummate poet. His songs are not the mere barbaric babble of crude emotions that might be expected from men of a culture labelled 'primitive'; they are clear-cut gems of diction, polished and repolished with loving care, according to the canons of a technique as exacting as it is beautiful.

That technique has been elaborated by centuries of singing ancestors who, sincerely convinced of beauty, enlisted every artifice of balance, form and rhythm to express it worthily. The island poet thrills as subtly as our own to the exquisite values of words, labouring as patiently after the perfect epithet. As a result, his songs are literature, though they have remained from the beginning unwritten.

I cannot here give details of the technique that the poet must master, or reproduce the sonorous music of the language he uses. At most, with the help of translated passages, I can hope to convey some faint idea of his results. Translation is the ultimate test of poetry. If, transposed to a foreign idiom and shorn of all its native rhythm, it has still 'a voice to search the heart,' then it is without any doubt true poetry.

Haste, ah, haste thee from the East, my beloved.
Thou has come out of bondage in Tonga,
Thou art gone like a tempest over the land;
Even the waves of the sea shrink back before thy wrath;

Thou comest in anger, thou Terrible One, yet I fear thee
   not.

Haste, ah, haste thee from the East, my beloved.
Thou art exalted in thine anger, thou are exalted in Tonga;
Thou treadest upon the clouds—they are tangled about
   thy feet;
Thou pluckest down with thy fingers the mountains of
   Samoa;
Yet thy hand upon my breast will be gentle as a child's.

Haste, ah, haste thee from the East my beloved.
Thy feet are swifter in the East than the feet of the wind
   and the rain;
The noise of thy coming is the tumult of falling skies;
So that in the face of all men thou art terrible,
Save only in my sight, who love thee, therefore fear not.

That is a song put into the mouth of a fabulous island
heroine, whose love has escaped from captivity in Tonga.
Many such songs, of unknown authorship, have been handed
down from generation to generation, embedded in the tales of
love and adventure that the brown man never tires of telling.
In these tales, which are sometimes masterpieces of prose
poetry, the transition from narrative verse is always adroitly
managed, the hero or heroine breaking into song (as Shake-
speare's characters break into rhyme) at moments of high
dramatic tension.

   Here is a fragment of a dirge from another well-known
story; you are to imagine that a son, while walking with a
company of friends, has stumbled unawares upon the body of
his murdered father:

SON   How still, how still thou liest,
   My father, oh, my father, Nakana!
   (*Aside*) Alas! Is the ghost gone out of him?
FRIENDS   The ghost is gone out of him.

O   201

ṢON Nakana! I call thy name. Thou speakes not Nakana.
Thy eyes look up to me but see me not.

(*Aside*) He stirs not. Will he nevermore stir?

FRIENDS The ghost is gone out of him.

SON Oh, dead eyes, light again. Behold my tears to
brighten you.

Oh, still breast, stir again. Behold my breath to move you.

(*Aside*) He stirs not. Will he nevermore stir?

FRIENDS The ghost is gone out of him.

SON Oh, cold body, take the warmth of my own flesh;

Thou who gavest me life, take back thy gift and live again.

(*Aside*) Will not even this awaken him?

Even so short an extract shows the poet's quality. Here
is a most compelling blend of artlessness and art. The perfect
and unstrained simplicity of the son's lament is enormously
dramatized by a flawless symmetry of structure. In each
strophe of the poem the mourner's cry is made the more
pathetic by his renewed appeal for comfort to the living, and
the pitifulness of the tragedy is stressed by the inexorable
reiterance of that refrain 'The ghost is gone out of him.'
The poet responsible for these lines was an artist penetrated by
his theme, in absolute control of his medium, and informed to
his inmost fibre with the magic of form and balance.

And here is a Gilbertese lover singing of his mistress:

How deep are my thoughts as I sit on the point of the land
Thinking of her tonight.
Her feet are luminous over dark ways,
Even as the moon stepping between clouds.
Her shoulders shine like Kaama in the South[1]
Her hands, in the sitting dance,
Trouble my eyes as the flicker of stars;
And at the lifting of her eyes to mine I am abashed,
I, who have looked undaunted into the sun.

[1] Southern Cross

202

My friend Taata, who, during my years there, was the greatest living poet of the Gilbert Islands, said to me once, "If I did not with heart and body live the life of my people, how could I sing songs to touch their hearts?"

That was his way of asserting that if poetry is to appeal to the people, it must savour of the salt of the people's life. His theory will not sound greatly amiss to lovers of Burns or Mistral, Chaucer or Hans Sachs; and, right or wrong, it has been the conviction of every poet who ever sang in the Gilbert Islands.

The singer of the Central Pacific is no aloof or lily-handed dreamer, who whiles away the languid hours:

In gardens near the pale of Proserpine,

. . . . . .

Where only the low lutes of love complain,
And only shadows of wan lovers pine.

He is a toiler, a son of sea and soil, a peasant poet. Hard manual labour is the keynote of his life. If it were not so, he would starve, for on the sunscorched atolls that are the home of his race, there is none of that tropical luxuriance of vegetation that novelists love to describe. There are but two trees that yield him food—the coconut and the pandanus palm—and in that arid soil it is only by incessant travail that he can keep them productive. Every day, too, in every weather, he must go out with net or line to wrest from perhaps the most treacherous seas in all the world the fish that forms his only other food.

According to Taata, the poet should excel all other men in performance of these labours. Only by becoming a recognized master of the island crafts can he win reverence for his art. His ideal is therefore to be a perfect man, as manhood is conceived in the Central Pacific.

So it comes about that the champion wrestlers and canoe-men, the most valiant warriors, the hardiest shark-fishers, the most skilful builders and agriculturalists in the annals of the Gilbertese race have been poets. In these islands, the dreamers of dreams are the men of action too.

It is only when the poet feels the divine spark of inspiration once more stirring within him that he deviates from the ordinary course of village life. Then indeed he neglects his digging and fishing, but only to subject himself to a far sterner discipline. He removes himself to some lonely spot, there to avoid all contact with man or woman. He eats nothing but the flesh of coconuts, and drinks nothing but water.

For three days he thus purges his body of its vicious humours. On the fourth morning he marks out a twelve-foot square on the ground, in some place where he can get a good view of the rising sun. This is his 'house of song,' wherein he will sit in travail with the poem that is yet unborn. All the next night he squats there, bolt upright, facing east, while the song quickens within him.

Dawn breaks. As the edge of the sun's disc appears over the eastern sea, the poet lifts his hands at arm's-length before him, with palms turned outwards to the rising flame:

"O, Sun," he intones, "thou art reborn out of darkness;
Thou comest out of deep places, thou comest out of
the terrible shadows;
Thou wast dead, thou art alive again.
O, Sun, behold me, help me:
The word of power died in my heart,
Let it be reborn again as thou,
Let it fill me with light as thou,
Let it soar above the shadows,
Let it live!
So shall I be eloquent."

This incantation (age-old inheritance from his magic-loving ancestors) he repeats three times, then rinses his mouth with

salt water, thereby making his tongue 'pure for song.' Immediately after this ritual, he goes to his village to seek five
friends. When he has found them he brings them back to
his 'house of song.' They carry with them as many withered
dancing wreathes as they can collect, together with the
feathers of frigate birds, and of this strange fuel they make a
small, acridly smoking fire in the middle of the 'house.'
The poet sits, in such a position that the smoke may be blown
upon him by the breeze, and his five friends face him in a
semicircle on the other side of the fire.

Without further preamble, he begins to recite the 'rough
draft' of his poem, which he has ruminated overnight. It is
the business of his friends to interrupt, criticize, interject
suggestions, applaud, or howl down, according to their taste.
Very often they do howl him down, too, for they are themselves poets. On the other hand, if the poem, in their opinion,
shows beauty they are indefatigable in abetting its perfection.
They will remain without food or drink under the pitiless
sun until night falls, searching for the right word, the balance,
the music that will convert it into a finished work of art.

When all their wit and wisdom has been poured out upon
him, they depart. He remains alone again—probably for
several days—to reflect upon their advice, accept, reject,
accommodate, improve, as his genius dictates. The responsibility for the completed song will be entirely his.

Like the songs of the old English 'makers,' of the French
troubadours, of the German minnesingers, Gilbertese poetry is
nearly all vocal in character. Usually, too, its proper accom-
paniment is the dance, for it is intensely dramatic.

Before a poem can come before the public, therefore, it
must be fitted to a chant, and interpreted in terms of movement by the sinuous and poised gestures of skilled dancers.
The adaptation of words to movement is called, for obvious
reasons, the 'Raising of the Hands.' Unless the poet be
himself an expert in this art, he must hand over his work to a
committee of 'producers,' past masters of dancing, who, for no

reward save honour, will elaborate the exquisitely difficult and intricate movements of torso, head, eyes, arms, and fingers intended to interpret the artist's theme.

Before this august body the village dancers assemble, perhaps two hundred strong, and phrase by phrase they learn the new song. As each passage becomes known, the experts sketch out the appropriate attitudes, which are tried and retried until satisfaction is reached. There are interminable repetitions, recapitulations, revisions, until the flesh is weary and the chant sickeningly familiar. But from a ragged performance of ill-timed voices and uncertain attitudes, the song-dance becomes a magnificent harmony of bodies, eyes and arms swinging and undulating in perfect attunement through a thousand poises, to the organ tone of ten score voices chanting in perfect rhythm. Then dawns the poet's day of glory.

The dance chants cover the whole range of experience that may befall an island people. They are heroic, celebrating warriors and travellers; elegiac, mourning the dead; lyrical, singing of love; and humorous, burlesquing men or manners. Even poems which profess to be nothing but farcical are worthy of serious attention, for they often delight one with satirical passages of a shrewd childlike penetration, and sometimes achieve epigram in the authentic manner of Martial—as in this scrap of a modern song:

> That man came shouting, "I am a chief."
> Certainly he looks lazy enough for the title;
> He also has the appetite of a king's son,
> And a very royal waddle.
> But he shouts, "I am a chief";
> Therefore I know he is not one.

This is the sort of sally which particularly delights the humour of a Gilbertese audience.

But you come upon sudden beauty too in these comic songs,

that soothes the senses as the trilling of a bird heard through the clatter of a farmyard. Here is a stave of pure music, which I found sandwiched between passages of not very decent buffoonery:

Whence camest thou, my sister? Tell me for I would hear.
Thou camest on a laggard wind, a day of baffling calms.
Thou hast brought unease to the land. My dreams are
     heavy,
For thou has brought the sickness of love to me.
Would I had never seen thy face! I love thee, I love thee!

The island singer knows full well that beauty is never out of place. And he realizes also that there is no 'leaden metal' that his alchemy cannot 'into gold transmute,' no subject however humble that cannot be turned into song, and no song, if it expresses the heart, that cannot outlive the years of a man and the ravages of time. Perhaps the song for the marriage of 'Movement of Clouds' and of the fulfilment of Old Eri's prophecy when a new home was found for his descendants, will be sung long after the facts are forgotten.

When, early in 1932, I was transferred to islands on the other side of the world and the time came for me to leave the Gilbert Islanders for good, I left their problems in other hands but I kept their songs: and amongst them was one that my friend Taata gave me:

Even in a little thing
(A leaf, a child's hand, a star's flicker)
I shall find a song worth singing
If my eyes are wide, and sleep not.

Even in a laughable thing
(Oh, hark! The children are laughing!)
There is that which fills the heart to overflowing,
And makes dreams wistful.

Small is the life of a man
(Not too sad, not too happy):
I shall find my songs in a man's small life. Behold
    them soaring!
Very low on earth are the frigate-birds hatched,
Yet they soar as high as the sun.

I was too busy obeying orders and learning about people in my apprentice days to be worrying much about what the Colonial Office really did mean by that terrifying phrase 'qualities of leadership,' and kind Mr. Johnson had retired by the time I got back to London. I never heard the answer; but I do not think it matters, because whatever the official ideal of leadership may have been in 1913, it is doubtless as dead today as the old imperialism that fostered it. The Heaven-born Big-White-Master theory of colonial administration began to crack up generously with the publication of Lord Lugard's epoch-making *Dual Mandate* in 1921, and great influences in the Colonial Office were pushing open back-doors in Whitehall for its relegation to viewless junk-yards during the late 'twenties and early 'thirties of the century.

It was in about the early 'thirties that officers of my genera-tion in the Pacific were first really prodded into sitting up and taking notice that our duty as officials was to operate less like the rulers, and more like the stewards, of the people among whom we worked. I cannot remember that the ideal of stewardship was ever propounded to us in so many words as an official doctrine. I don't think it ever was. It merely integrated itself in our minds from the changed nature of the orders we received from Downing Street. These not only told us in greater detail than ever before what to do and how to do it, but they called for results, and reports upon results into the bargain. Their insistences drilled us into accepting a part of our minimum routine a number of field activities which, until then, had been left very much to our personal choice. Our service began to look more like a service and less like a squirearchy. In short, we had to hop around doing things for the simple sake of being worth the salaries the local tax-payers paid us. It was very good for all of us, from Governors down to cadets.

The new philosophy filtered through to us over the next few years in varying states of dilution or concentration. Political changes at home were not the only reason for that. There was also a tough Old Guard of senior officials both in Whitehall and in the field who did not take kindly to the accelerated decay of the proconsular tradition. But there was continual pressure for the review, and revision, and more vigorous administration of laws affecting the fundamental rights of underprivileged peoples. We groaned at the endless questionnaires; we pointed out that dozens of its assumptions were false, scores of its suppositions mere mare's-nests; and what we said was often true; half the stuff that came down to us was grotesquely wide of the mark. But the other half went straight to the bull's-eye. The circular instructions on a vast range of subjects addressed to Governors in the field played a critical part in educating all of us up to a modern view of our colonial obligations.

As early as 1936, long forward strides in the delegation of power to colonial peoples began to be taken. From that year onwards, the official *blocs* which had traditionally dominated the vote in many local legislatures began to be cut down to three members and superseded by large majorities of non-officials. Wherever that has been achieved (and the pace and scope of reforms have increased much of late) the Governor of a colony no longer operates as the celestial autocrat of his political breakfast-table. Apart from the exercise of his strictly bridled reserve powers—which happens once in a blue moon—the enormous majority of his business is confined to administering the government within the limits of local laws passed by the representatives of the people. In effect, where once his sole ultimate obligations were to take orders from a supercelestial Secretary of State sitting in Whitehall and to see that the official *bloc* passed them into law, he now owes a twofold loyalty. On one side, he is still the servant of the United Kingdom which appointed him; on the other, he is the servant of the community whose free vote provides his salary and finances the public service which he controls.

The old imperialism never did want for Governors and field-officers eager to lend themselves wholly to the service of the peoples they were sent to rule. But that was the greatness of the men, not of the system. The truest kind of leadership in those days was to be one of an almost forgotten host working in the colonies to give the lie by tacit example to every truculence of the Jingo doctrine. Not the imperialism of Britain, but the liberalism of individual Britons, plugging along at their jobs in the field, was the force that held the affections of simple peoples true to the mother-country throughout the long era of autocratic rule.

In its own way our system worked, on the whole, with real benevolence among simple peoples. When we got into the field we saw it inspiring many of our senior officers to earnest work, and often deep self-sacrifice, in desolate places. We took these as our heroes and tried to follow in their footsteps. It was very seldom that we ran up against an open difference of opinion between an unsophisticated population and Whitehall. When we did, we took it for granted that somebody must eventually play the part of the good little boy, and that this somebody mustn't—couldn't possibly be—a Secretary of State (or even an Assistant Under Secretary of State) for the Colonies. It was our job to convey this politely to our villagers, and we generally managed to do so because they truly were our friends. We did not stop to think then how much more the maintenance of Pax Britannica owed to their marvellous patience and courtesy with us than to the inherent virtue of ourselves or our system.

As cadets, we had to pass examinations in native languages, which opened the door to personal conversation with the people. There was much house-to-house visitation in the villages, and we did try to learn a little about native customs; but when it came to manners, we felt that here was a subject which we had to teach rather than learn. Setting aside high ceremonial occasions, it occurred to few European officers of the day that their own behaviour as guests could possibly be criticized by their village hosts.

I often heard authority say in those days that sympathy is a quality which cannot be taught, anyhow, to officers who have it not within them. That was the usual starting-point for criticism of plans to improve our understanding of colonial populations through the teaching of ethnology and history. It took some time for us to worry out our answers. The one that I always liked best was that what most men need or expect from their neighbours in any environment is not a diurnal gush of sympathetic emotion over the hedge, but just a silent respect for their private occasions. Romans are ultimately convinced of the stranger's goodwill towards them, not by the extent to which he does as Romans do, but by the extent to which he avoids treading upon their innocent grass-plots. Workaday sympathy for neighbours is, in fact, most commonly expressed through a number of civilized avoidances, which are usually drilled into one during childhood by a series of fundamental DON'Ts. The very least that ethnology and history have to teach any colonial administrative service is a list of such local DON'Ts. On that minimum claim alone they qualify for the attention of anyone—whether administrator, or missionary, or business man—who really wants to be accepted as a desirable import by the colonial community of his choice.

As time went on, we were encouraged to take up ethnology more seriously by the establishment of courses in that subject for administrative recruits in England. But I think that the generality of us went on for a long time looking upon the study of native custom rather as a pleasantly recondite personal hobby than as a means of getting down to the bedrock of a people's will to live, work and develop under the impact of European ideas. To borrow the memorable phrase of an African spokesman recently heard on the air, our kindness consisted mostly of treating local populations as babies to be spoonfed, whether they liked the spoon or not. Generally speaking, we were earnest in the delegation of authority by limited instalments on the lines of Lord Lugard's teaching. But I must admit that the policy appealed to us most of all as a convenient device for enlisting the collaboration of local bodies in our particular way of cultivating the imperial rosegarden. Some time was to pass before we began to look upon it as a technique for the gradual transfer of political initiative from ourselves to them. Our official ideal, in the last analysis, was to rule rather than to find out how far the people's national genius could be canalized or developed in the direction of selfrule.

'Partnership' is now the word used to define Britain's relationship with her colonies. It is a good word to connote the just balance of initiative between home and colonial governments, pending a time when full autonomy for all can be achieved. But it fails entirely to cover the functions or motives of the intermediary between the partners—the Colonial Service, as such. Co-equal partners may deal in government, but the service in their dual employ simply serves. Colonial administrations today are agents, not rulers. Stewardship is their ultimate business in the field, and it is part of their stewardship to keep their employers—Britain on one hand, the colonies of their service on the other—on constant terms of mutual understanding and sympathy. Theirs is a continuous, two-way, holding-together service of representation and interpretation. There never was an age when they wielded less political power or had the chance to wield so mighty a personal influence for political peace and human unity.

Because of the loss of political initiative and the increase of psychological responsibility (or, as I privately and sentimentally prefer to say, because now not heads and hands alone, but hearts also must be officially engaged in the work of stewardship), the personal capacity of the administrative officer in the field to understand and interpret his community is today more important than ever it was before. The Colonial Office has recognized the demand and risen to it. Its courses of training for aspirants to colonial service have been profoundly and, as I think, nobly refashioned of late. The intentions of the courses established at Oxford, Cambridge and London are to send out young men educated in political and economic subjects, endowed with an ideal of inter-departmental team-work in the field, pre-sensitized to the cultures of the peoples they are to serve, and inspired with a will to speed forward the enlistment of local genius in the development of free local institutions.

Voices have been raised to conjecture drearily that the courses may flood the colonies with a breed of arrogant young doctrinaires, impatient of the slowness of simple peoples in responding to schemes devised for their own benefit. Pups, in short, just as my Old Man of Ocean Island was calling me and my species all those years ago. The Old Guard dies hard and its criticisms always carefully sidestep every vital, heartening fact. The main fact about the present training scheme is, of course, that it stands for an official ideal of administration fit at last to inspire a whole Service instead of leaving the Service to be uplifted, as of old, only here and there from within itself by a leaven of inspired officers. This is leadership coming from the right direction—the top—the Colonial Office, and it is enough, by my reckoning, to send young men into the field today a great deal less puzzled about the leaderly qualities expected of them than I was in 1913.